Emotional Intelligence for Women

Improve your communication skills, leadership and self confidence for relationship, work and business

By Donna Mayer

Table of Contents

Introduction

In the world of work today, women are still finding themselves lagging behind men in pay scale but more importantly, in opportunities. No matter how badly a woman might want to inhabit the plush corner office, the bulk of those opportunities are still going to male employees. Women need a new tactic to utilize to get the types of career positions they are ready for now.

In *Emotional Intelligence for Women* by Donna Mayer, the author gives women exactly the secret weapon they need to be highly successful in the modern world. That secret weapon is emotional intelligence. Women do not yet realize that they have been groomed from birth to be more emotionally intelligent than men and once they learn the tricks of this secret weapon, there will be no holding the women back anymore.

Emotional intelligence will allow women to use the skills they have been using for centuries as tools to climb the corporate ladder and get the key to that office. Since women have already been using this secret weapon in many other ways, it should be an easy matter for them to translate the results of this skill into skills for the world of work.

And since this skill is easily translated into other areas of the woman's life, it will be a simple matter to use these tactics in everything the woman is involved in, such as personal relationships, roommate situations, and life events involving the children. This skill will make women more confident and capable and will enable her to be more socially competent than ever before.

And since women are predisposed to be able to use this skill very well at any time they want to, there is no better time to begin than now.

Chapter 1: What Is Emotional Intelligence?

Emotional intelligence, simply defined, is the ability to know, understand, control, use, and express personal emotions in order to be able to maintain relationships with other people and to do so empathetically and judiciously. It is the ability to know that actions are driven by emotions and that those emotions in other people can be used to better one's own position. People are affected by emotions, both negatively and positively, and people can learn how to manage their emotions.

Being able to manage one's emotions is important during times of stress and change when dealing with failure and setbacks when embroiled in challenging relationships, when receiving or giving feedback, or when personal resources are limited, and creativity must be used in order to survive and succeed. Emotional intelligence consists of being able to use these three skills: It is the ability to identify and understand one's own personal emotions; the knowledge to be able to use those emotions when problem-solving or brainstorming, and; the internal power to use personal emotions and the emotions of others whenever needed.

This does not necessarily mean that an emotionally intelligent woman is totally devoid of emotion. Rather it is the ability to manage and identify emotions. An emotionally intelligent woman is quite conscious of her own emotions, even the negative ones. And she is able to sense feeling in another person and has the power to use their emotions to gain her goal. This begins with self-awareness.

Personal self-awareness is the cornerstone of growth and success in one's personal life and the professional world. It is impossible to be emotionally intelligent without first being aware of what drives us emotionally. You must be able to see and understand your own emotions and accept them for what they are. You must realize that you alone have the power to control your emotions. When you begin to analyze your feelings and thoughts, and understand them better, you will begin to be able to have control over them instead of the other way around. You will be able to rule your emotions.

It is definitely not necessary to immediately react to every emotion and every event. You have the ability to choose which stimuli will cause you to act and which ones you will ignore. But to be able to do this, you must first admit that you have emotions and that those emotions are really good useful things. Once you begin to choose exactly how you will and will not respond, you begin to have control over your personal emotions. When your emotions rule you, then you are a prisoner of your own thoughts, and you will never have the freedom you deserve.

		Recognition	Regulation
Personal Competence		**Self-Awareness** ✓ Self-confidence ✓ Awareness of your emotional state ✓ Recognizing how your behavior impacts others ✓ Paying attention to how others influence your emotional state	**Self-Management** ✓ Getting along well with others ✓ Handling conflict effectively ✓ Clearly expressing ideas and information ✓ Using sensitivity to another person's feelings (empathy) to manage interactions successfully
Social Competence		**Social Awareness** ✓ Picking up on the mood in the room ✓ Caring what others are going through ✓ Hearing what the other person is "really" saying	**Relationship Management** ✓ Getting along well with others ✓ Handling conflict effectively ✓ Clearly expressing ideas/information ✓ Using sensitivity to another person's feelings (empathy) to manage interactions successfully

Initial   Self   –   Analysis

Becoming more aware of your limits and your strengths will make you more confident in your abilities and what you are and are not able to do. People who are naturally self-confident have the power to be assertive in their words and actions. It does not mean that you will win every situation. It does mean that you are able to share your feelings and thoughts confidently and you are able to convey to others what you think is right and why you feel that way.

An awareness of your emotions can be developed. Take some time to think about your emotional responses and look for areas that you handle well and areas that need improvement. Make a list so that you have concrete evidence in front of you when you are working on you. Write down your personal strengths and weaknesses and rate each one. Ask other people to help you rate yourself if you like. Be prepared to hear things you might not want to hear. Use an online personality test if you like.

You will begin to work on your personal emotions based on the list of emotions you have written down. Start keeping a journal of your daily interactions with others and the feelings you had during each encounter. Keep track of how you react during certain situations, including any physical reactions you might have. Sometimes emotional responses appear as physical symptoms. Consider how you fit into all the personal relationships you deal with on a regular basis. Women wear many hats. They are wives, sisters, daughters, mothers, employers, or employees. They can be athletes, instructors, writers, or musicians. Keep track of different situations and how you feel when you are in certain roles. Then you can play "what if" with your emotions. Before you go into a certain situation, ask yourself how you think it might play out and how you might feel. Ask yourself how you plan to react to different scenarios. If you can distinguish the feeling that you might be feeling in the situation, then you have become aware of your emotions, and you are taking steps to control them.

Once you have become aware of your own emotions, then you can learn to manage them. It is a normal human reaction to say the wrong thing at the wrong time when emotions are running high. Usually, by the time most people realize they have overreacted to the situation, the damage is already done. You have already sent the email with the message you could have said more tactfully. Or, you have already hurt the feelings of someone you really do love. And you can't possibly take the words back once they are said.

The opposite of this is what happens all too often when people are well aware that they tend to say the wrong thing at the wrong time, so they say nothing. The anxiety and fear that comes from being afraid to say the wrong thing grips like a vise and people just remain silent, completely losing the opportunity to speak or act when we know we should. Freezing up can bring consequences that are even worse than overreacting. Whichever way the pendulum swings, getting a grip on personal emotions is sometimes not the easiest thing to do.

The answer is almost always the same. People blame their emotions for overtaking them. But then, that brings the question of exactly who is in charge. Are you in charge of your own emotions, or are they in charge of you? Most people are raised without ever being taught how to manage their emotions. They reach adulthood with raging hormones and emotions and have no clue what to do with them. If we are taught anything as a child, it is to bury any negative emotions that might come up and never, ever act on them. Other people then say that it is bad to hide emotions, and people should feel free to let everything out in the open.

In order to be able to manage our emotions, we need to understand a few truths about them. We must be willing to acknowledge that emotions will rise whether we want them to or not. We can't turn them off and on like a faucet on the sink. When you accept this fact, then you will be able to understand that negative emotions won't just go away. You will also be able to accept the fact that your emotions will become stronger with every step you take toward living your life according to your particular values and beliefs. As your positive emotions become stronger, your negative emotions will become stronger also; it is almost a battle of wills.

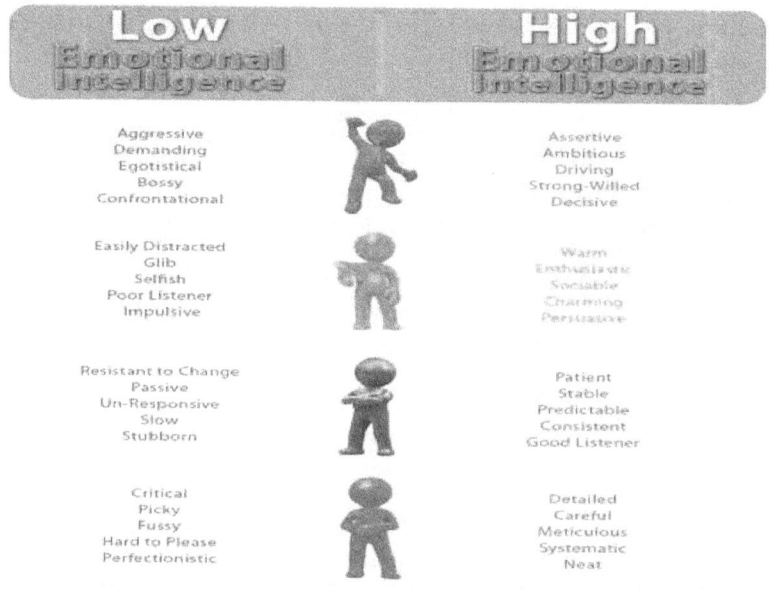

Low Emotional Intelligence	High Emotional Intelligence
Aggressive Demanding Egotistical Bossy Confrontational	Assertive Ambitious Driving Strong-Willed Decisive
Easily Distracted Glib Selfish Poor Listener Impulsive	Warm Enthusiastic Sociable Charming Persuasive
Resistant to Change Passive Un-Responsive Slow Stubborn	Patient Stable Predictable Consistent Good Listener
Critical Picky Fussy Hard to Please Perfectionistic	Detailed Careful Meticulous Systematic Neat

Low Emotional Intelligence Vs High Emotional Intelligence

And even though emotions are referred to as positive and negative, no emotion is either bad or good. An emotion simply exists. Those emotions that we try to resist will only become stronger. The key is to allow ourselves to feel all human emotions without calling them good or bad. Being able to accept this is supremely liberating for our souls. When we are able to accept our emotions as a part of our makeup, we can begin to exert control over them.

There will always be a choice for us to make. Having a feeling or thought does not keep you from committing to an action. Just think of the emotion as a trick the mind plays, like when you feel fear and are unable to speak or move. It is better to accept and acknowledge the emotion and admit that you feel fear, so you chose not to speak. In that way, you are taking control of the emotion, rather admitting that the emotion is controlling you. When we are able to see our emotions as a vital part of ourselves, then we will be able to choose how we decide to react to them. This brings us to the place where we begin to take responsibility for our emotions.

When our emotions rise, the body will give off clues that you have an emotional reaction. Your head might begin to pound, your pulse might start racing, and your face may feel flushed. These are physical clues to the turmoil going on in your mind, and by looking for them, you give yourself the chance to know the emotional rise is coming and the opportunity to control your reaction. You will need to have a strong will to be able to stop yourself because this skill will take constant practice to develop, but it is well worth the fight. Once you have identified the emotional reaction, you can do something to distract yourself until the feeling passes. After the strongest part of the reaction is over, you are able to consider the emotions involved, decide what made you feel them, and plan ways to proceed in the future, so that your reactions might not be so strong. This is the first step toward controlling your emotions.

Along with learning to control our own emotions, we must be able to understand the emotions of other people in order to foster good relationships with others. In order to be able to improve our relationships with other people, we must develop the ability to feel sympathy for their emotions while still controlling our own reactions. This is called feeling empathy for the other person. Empathy is the ability to show that we understand the other person's feelings by drawing on a similar situation we once had. We will learn why they feel this way and how they came to feel this way by attempting to see the situation from the other person's point of view. It is impossible to feel empathy without having a good level of self-awareness of the emotions that we feel because empathy requires that we relate to the other person on a very personal level.

When another person begins to share their feelings about their particular situation, then you begin to search in your subconscious for a similar incident so that your brain knows which emotions to act on. It is a way to put yourself in the shoes of the other person. It does not mean that you agree with all that they are feeling and thinking. It only means that you can see the situation from the point of view of the other person. Being able to do this will build trust in other people toward   you.

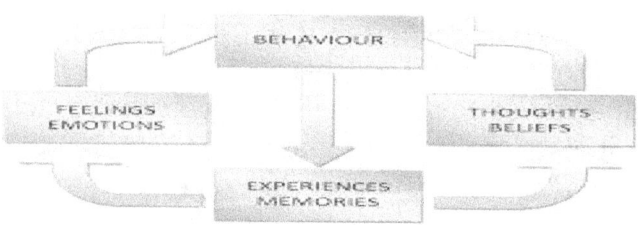

Empathy is an emotion that can be learned. You will start by trying to put yourself in the other person's place; see what they might be experiencing. Look for similarities between yourself and the other person. Try to develop a real feeling of interest in the lives and emotions of those around you. Think about situations you might have heard about and try to decide how you would react in the same situation. Listen when other people are talking. That means to really hear what they are saying and not just wait for your turn to speak. Never make generalities about other people. When thoughts arise that begin with "someone always" or "someone never," then stop and rewrite those phrases in your mind. You might ask one or two trusted friends to watch your progress and give you feedback.

Developing empathy for others is the first step in developing good social skills. Good social skills are a mandatory part of emotional intelligence. Remember that all emotional intelligence really means is the ability to manage your own emotions and react properly to the emotions that other people display. These are people who are able to keep their personal emotions from flowing over and taking over their lives, being able to read others and respond to their needs, and being able to manage personal conflict. Being competent socially is much more than just being able to carry on a conversation with other people, although that is an important component of having good social skills.

Having a basic skill level for communicating with others will give you the ability to follow directions, speak when it is your turn, and being able to really listen to other people. You will show others that you are listening by your body language, like nodding and making eye contact. When your turn comes to speak repeat part of what they said back to them; this shows that you were really paying attention to what they said.

In addition to developing good communication skills, it is necessary to develop good interpersonal skills. This means being able to join activities, share with others, taking your turn, and asking permission. If you are not able to ask a simple question of another person, then you will not be able to initiate simple conversations or gain information from others. People who struggle with communication will be seen as anti-social or not interested in others. This will also affect your abilities to solve problems because you may choose to ignore the problem instead of trying to correct it.

It is possible to gain good social skills by simply engaging in three processes. These are seeing what is happening, thinking about what is happening, and then doing something about what is happening. Examine the social cues you see and determine what you can about the situation. Think about what these cues are telling you about the situation. Then once you have analyzed the situation, act upon what you see and think to be true in a way that is positive.

The basic life skills that lead up to the ability to have emotional intelligence are generally learned during childhood, almost from birth. This is where people begin to develop their personal thought processes, and it influences how they see the world. These stages were first identified during the 1930's, and the theories are still widely used today. The basis of this developmental theory is that children use their life experiences to create their own knowledge of the world, children easily learn things without being formally taught by others, and children naturally love to learn.

As children grow from birth, they pass through several stages of life development. During roughly the first two years, a child learns basically just motor skills. They learn how to navigate, literally, and everything is based on their own trial and error. So when they learn to crawl, walk, talk, and eat with a spoon, they will try different methods to see which one really works. Between ages two and seven, the child is developing imagination and memory. Children in this age group tend to see everything from their own point of view; they are the star of the show. Children of this age group are learning that everything has a name, even feelings and emotions, and they are learning the names that go with objects and emotions. From age seven to 11, the child learns that they can begin to manipulate what they see as symbols, such as the symbols for emotions. They learn that they can act sad or act happy and invoke a certain response from people. They will use their thoughts to begin to see not only their own place in the world but also how they can influence the world through their own behavior. After age 11, children merely get better at their manipulation skills as they become more mature in their practice. These are not the manipulation skills that people usually think of when they think of someone being manipulative. These are the skills that will bring the child to a level of emotional intelligence where they will be able to control their emotions and use them in a proper manner in the world at large.

People learn in set patterns, much like the brain is reading an instructional card for an activity. Think of going to the grocery store to pick up a few items. You do not think about entering the store, walking through the aisles, picking up the needed items, checking out, and then leaving. The brain remembers all this for you and guides your body to perform properly even if your conscious mind is not in control. Once we have learned these patterns, then our brains will assimilate and accommodate.

We assimilate when we use a learned pattern for a new situation. Pretend you are taking care of two babies of the same age. One baby cries and you give it a bottle; magically the baby stops crying, so you assume it was just hungry. Now baby number two starts crying and you give it a bottle but the baby refuses it. You used assimilation to take an existing idea and apply it to a new situation: give the baby a bottle, and it will stop crying. But it did not work with baby number two, so now what?

Now you accommodate. The plan you had in mind did not work with the second baby, so your brain must create a new plan. This is when you try different methods to make the baby stop crying, such as hold it, change it and burp it. All of these things your brain knows from past experience, so you draw on that experience to create a new plan.

This is the basis of emotional intelligence. We learn how certain emotions can be used in ways that are positive and negative. Emotional intelligence uses trial and error to learn what emotions work best in certain situations. Since cognitive intelligence generally refers to things that are learned, it can easily be translated to the world of emotions and emotional intelligence. If people learn how to tie their shoes and how to boil water, then they are able to learn how to control their emotions in social situations and how to use their emotions in a positive way to gain control of the situations they find themselves in throughout life.

Success in life comes from many different factors and emotional intelligence is one of the most critical that a person can learn. Beginning with being aware of one's own emotions and learning how to manage emotions in different situations, all the way through using emotions properly in social situations and learning good social skills, emotional intelligence is the key that will bring the end results desired in life.

Chapter 2: Are Women More Emotionally Intelligent Than Men?

Most of the tests that are currently being used to grade emotional intelligence suggest that women exceed men in overall emotional intelligence. There are some areas where men outscore women, as in when it comes to managing emotions that are brought on by sadness or distress. When scientists compare gender differences in emotional development between men and women, they are referring to two different curves that largely overlap each other—one being for men and the other being for women. This simply means that any one woman might be just as good as any one man at handling various emotional issues.

One area where women are better than men is in the area of feeling empathy. There are actually three parts to the emotion of empathy. You must be able to see things the way the other person sees them. You must be able to feel the emotion that the other person is feeling, and you must be sympathetic and ready to help the person who needs help. In general, women are much better at empathy than men are.

Women complain that men are unemotional creatures, and men complain that women are overly emotional, and both statements are true to a certain point. When men feel empathy, they only feel it for a moment; then the feeling disappears as it is replaced by the problem-solving part of their brain that wants to fix things. Women's brains hold onto the feelings of empathy much longer than men's brains do. This is partly why women have, for so long, been the workforce that becomes nurses, teachers, and counselors because women can feel what the other person is feeling and then act on that feeling to remedy the situation. Women are able to feel and solve where men's brains automatically jump to solve the problem.

An alternate way to view at this is to compare the male brain syndrome with the female brain syndrome. What scientists refer to as the female brain is a brain that is high in emotional empathy, whereas, a male brain is seen to be higher in analyzing and problem-solving. This does not mean that anyone needs to strictly fall into one category or the other. This is just the way used to describe the two different fields of thought. Top leaders in any field need to be proficient at both feeling and thinking. But women may be inherently better at using emotional intelligence than men are.

In order to conform to the scientific model of emotional intelligence, a person needs to have high abilities in four different areas. The first area is the perception of emotions, which is simply the ability to see and analyze emotional responses in voices, pictures, faces, and cultural artifacts. This is also the ability to be able to identify the emotions within oneself. It is impossible to achieve all the other elements of emotional intelligence without being able to perceive emotions. The ability to accurately use emotions for problem-solving and thinking is known as facilitation. This is the ability to use emotions in varying degrees in social situations, depending on the exact situation. The person who is emotionally intelligent will know that it is possible to use different emotions in different situations in order to best interact with others. Processing the basic language of emotions, including personal emotions, and knowing why certain emotions will cause people to act in a particular way is the ability to understand. This also includes the ability to detect small changes in other's emotions that might change the outcome of the situation at hand and knowing how emotions will change over a period of time or a particular set of circumstances. All these lead up to the ability to manage the emotions of self and the emotions of others in social situations. Those people who are seen to be emotionally intelligent has the innate ability to use whatever type of emotion present to their own best conclusion while pursuing their goals.

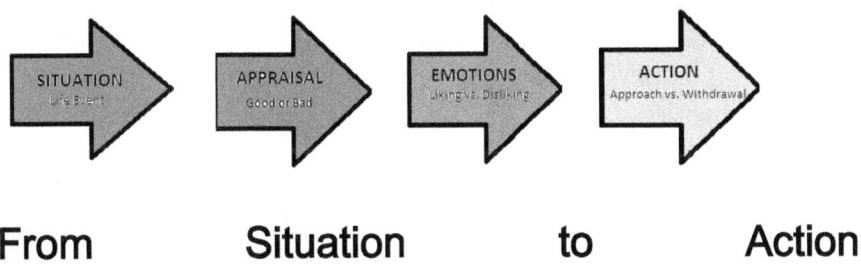

From   Situation   to   Action

With emotional perception, you are able to identify and recognize the emotions that others have as well as the physiological and biological process that is involved with emotions. When thinking about the impact that emotions have on everyday life, it is necessary to consider the cognitive appraisal, physical changes, and subjective experiences that emotions bring to a person. Possessing a good perception of emotions is having the ability to interpret the physical changes in another person made by the sensory systems that are responsible for changing these physical reactions into an emotion that you can see in your mind and make a decision about. Being able to see emotion in someone else is partly born into a person and partly learned through paying attention to one's surroundings. It social interactions it is critical to be good at perceiving emotions in others. Perception affects exactly how emotions are interpreted and perceived, and personal perception can be affected greatly by experiences from one's past.

Once you are able to read and sense emotions in other people and in yourself, you are in a position to begin to be able to use emotions to facilitate thinking. The word facilitates merely means to make something easier to do. So in being able to read emotions, it is easier to learn to use those emotions to one's own benefit. This is important for several reasons. Different states of emotion will work better with specific approaches to problems. Different moods and feelings will help you consider several different viewpoints. Memories of personal emotions can give a different opinion or judgment. And important information will be gained because your attention will be directed to a specific thought process according to the way you process emotions.

In working with different states of emotion to choose a specific approach, it is important to know how to deal with individual emotions. People who are angry are more likely to be risk takers than people who are in a good mood. People who are angry are more likely to act before thinking and to rely more on stereotypical ideas. Anger may require a special touch to be able to control. You want to harness the energy of the angry person without keeping them in an angry state.

Unfortunately, happy people do not always make good choices, either. People who are in a good mood are more likely to listen to lengthy messages whether they like the content or not. They will focus on how much they are enjoying being with the person giving the message and not so much on what the message contains. Happy people need to be dealt with differently than angry people. They need to have their level of happiness maintained while still understanding the message or the situation around them.

A certain level of sadness can be a good motivator because it causes the person to be thoughtful and to analyze the situation or the message. When none of the available options brings an instant hit of happiness, the person will spend more time weighing the pros and cons. But sadness as an emotion only works to a certain level of thought. Someone who is too deep in sadness will be unable to make a decision. And a deep level of sadness might make a person feel more impatient than other people in certain situations.

When dealing with different emotions in an attempt to use them for your own needs, it is important not to act immediately but to weigh the situation. It may be necessary to look at the situation from another point of view. Getting fired is devastating, but it might give you the option to start your own business or go back to school. It is also possible to take emotions out of the situation for long enough to make a decision. If you dearly love two houses and can't decide which one to buy, then remove the emotional factor and go with pros and cons, deciding which house better suits your needs at the time.

Keep in mind that your own emotions may cloud your judgment in a way that is not beneficial to the situation. Obviously, certain memories help to keep us safe. Remembering a near drowning will make you more cautious around water. A memory of touching the hot stove will cause you to be more careful when using the stove. These are needed emotions that keep you safe. When a memory clouds your emotions, it can cause you to make a bad decision. If one person of the opposite sex broke your heart, you can't look at all the members of the opposite sex as heartbreakers.

Seeing emotional responses and using them is impossible without actually being able to understand the emotions being presented. Emotions are important to everyday functioning. Our relationships with others are also affected by our emotions. The way you handle your emotions is important in how you will handle the emotions of others. If you do not understand your own emotions, then you will never understand the emotions of other people. So whenever you feel an emotion, take a moment to analyze it and seeing what it means to you. As soon as you identify the emotion in your own mind, think of more words that will serve to describe the emotion. Identifying the emotion will give it meaning to you and will give a starting point to work from in being able to use that emotion.

It is important to do this exercise with negative emotions and positive emotions alike. Once you identify the emotion, come up with synonyms to describe. If you are happy about a certain situation, then you can also be ecstatic, overjoyed, or exuberant. It is okay to call the emotion by the basic name everyone uses because those are likely to come to your mind first. But by giving the basic emotion more significance with a more descriptive word, you make it more important to your thought processes and more likely that you will recall that feeling when needed. Having the ability to put a name to an emotion will give you the ability to decide in advance your intentions for the relationship or the role and how it will work for you in the future. And when you are giving a name to your emotions, remember to give them an intensity number. Ask yourself how strong this emotion is to you. Emotions that are strongly felt are more likely to be recalled later and more likely to be helpful later.

It is beneficial to write down your emotional episodes in a notebook or a journal so that you are able to go back and review them later. Doing this will allow you to look at the situation and its emotions when you are not feeling that emotion quite so strongly. Perhaps you wrote about an event that made you so angry you could hardly see straight. You wrote fabulous synonyms for the word angry. Maybe you were irritated, inflamed, indignant, or exasperated. Looking at that same incident a few weeks later may make you see it in a different light when you aren't so angry in the heat of the moment. Maybe you would have approached the situation from a different angle. Maybe there was no need to be quite so angry. When you are logging your experiences, be sure to note what time of day the incident happened and any other significant events that are going on in your life. Maybe you weren't really that angry about the neighbor's dog running through your flowers. Maybe it was dinnertime, and you were hungry, or your teenager had put a dent in the car's back bumper earlier that day. Being honest with yourself and how and why you feel the way you do will be very important in helping you learn to understand the emotions of others.

And keeping track of your emotions does not mean just journaling the events that make you angry. All human emotion is important for proper mental function. Logging all types of events and emotions will make it easier for you to analyze and understand more situations and more about how you think. You might find that gardening really makes you ecstatically happy. And that feeling of regret and sadness you felt when you failed at your last home improvement project could give you the incentive to learn more about that process so that you can attempt it again and do a better job. It is all about learning and growing.

Once you have learned how to recognize, understand, and use emotions, you will be ready to begin managing them. Managing emotional responses is key to enjoying good relationships in any situation. Some emotional reaction is good, but people tend to stay away from those who are always so intense with their emotional reactions because such people tend to be exhausting. Some overreacting emotionally is normal. In the middle of an intense situation, people say things that they do not really mean to say. You answer an email by immediately responding with an angry and sarcastic email of your own without really considering the repercussions. This is why learning to manage emotions is so important because, by the time you have said or done something, it is said or done. You can't take it back. You will say or do something that offends someone at some time in your life, so you need to accept that fact and deal with it.

You will not be able just to repress unwanted emotions. It does not happen. You need to accept this fact so that you can begin the process of learning to manage your emotions. And try not to think of your emotions as negative or positive. If you label emotions as negative, the brain will attempt to stay away from those emotions because the brain is wired only to enjoy positive things. You will never learn to manage all of your emotions unless you are able to acknowledge their existence. Those things that you try to resist will continue to haunt you in ways you do not want. So accepting the existence of all human emotions will give you the ability to process them and the reactions they give you.

Never confuse yourself with your emotions. You are a unique person with commitments and values who has emotions that are sometimes strong and sometimes not quite appropriate for the situation. Your emotions have regular daily triggers that can be set off when you least expect it. It is important to realize this because if you allow yourself to be linked to your emotions, they become you and you are labeled by them. You become the angry person or the sad person, not the person who is sometimes angry and sometimes sad. Refusing to become your emotion means that your emotions will no longer control your behavior.

And there will always be a choice for you to make regarding your emotions. You are never prevented from committing an action just because of a feeling or a thought you have. It is normal for you to say to yourself that you are afraid of the consequences, so you decide not to speak or act. Change that thought to reflect the idea that you understand that you are afraid of the consequences and so you chose not to speak. This takes the control away from the emotion and gives it back to you. You now have a space in which to examine your personal values and commitments and decide how they fit into the situation. It is impossible always to choose the emotions that you have, but you are fully able to determine the reaction that you will have to those emotions.

Being human requires possessing emotions and, good or bad; these emotions are mostly the woman's domain. Stereotypically, women have been seen as the ones with all of the emotions. Women are considered to be unstable emotionally more often than men are. Women are often seen to be emotional during certain monthly times or moody for no reason. Women, much more than men, experience jealousy, despair, sadness, and anger. It is quite true that women are more emotional than men are. Our bodies are hard-wired to cry more easily and feel emotions more deeply. Society tells women that they need to nurture others and feel their emotions and men are supposed to do things and think deep thoughts. Men do have emotions but their emotional responses usually come out as anger.

Even though women are often seen as weak and unsuitable because they have emotions, those very emotions can be the driver that makes women more suited for success in society. Since women have the ability to sense other's emotions quickly and act upon what they sense, they have the innate ability to detect the unhappiness felt by colleagues and clients alike and to act on those feelings and make the situation better for all concerned. Being more people-oriented makes women a natural choice for situations that need team building or networking, among others.

Women generally deal with other people better because they are naturally empathic and compassionate. Being labeled as emotional creatures means that women are naturally good at building relationships with other people and winning people over to their side. While men are looking for the logic in the situation, women are trying to get everyone together on the same path toward the same goal.

So possessing and using emotions are not illogical and disruptive as we have been led to believe. Women must also learn to understand and manage their personal emotions so that they are not seen as unreasonable, illogical, irrational, or excessive. Women need to keep the focus on the desired goal and what it will take to reach that goal and not how it will feel along the way. This will give women the ability to harness the passion that naturally comes with emotional responses and use that passion to their advantage.

Women need to work on keeping inappropriate public emotions in private. Crying and similar emotional responses are quite normal, but they have no place in certain situations like work. These emotions are not inappropriate by themselves but are not appropriate in certain situations, and women need to learn these situations and develop steps to control their responses. Maybe they need to change the subject or step away from the situation for a while.

Women who learn how to harness their emotions and control them in all situations will naturally be successful in whatever they attempt. Emotions should be changed into good feelings as soon as possible and used to your advantage. Women who have control of their emotions and are good at practicing emotional intelligence will go far in life in whatever they attempt to do. Emotions are a great advantage when you know how to use them, and you use them well. Never feel that you need to shun or bury your emotions but rather learn to use them to your advantage. They will be your best weapon in life.

Chapter 3: Transforming Emotions into Emotional Intelligence

Human beings have emotions; that is a part of our lives that we cannot deny or ignore. Emotions have a role to play in every part of everyday life, even in the place where we work. People like to think that the tough people get moving when the way becomes tough, but the reality is that most people fall apart, at least momentarily, when things become more intense than we like them to be. People have outbursts of emotion all the time. They become frustrated, angry, or feel like crying. In today's workplace, where resources are often very low, and company expectations are very high, it is normal for people to be emotional now and then. A place of business without emotions is an unrealistic expectation.

Working at any business that frowns on the use of emotions is not a healthy place to be. It is not reasonable or healthy to think that it is possible never to show any type of emotion while at work. Many people are not able to walk the fine line that exists between being overly emotional and just emotional enough for the situation. This issue seems to pertain more to women than men because women are seen as more naturally emotional creatures. Women are sometimes considered to be unprofessional and weak in the workplace.

Both men and women have emotions, but women seem to exhibit more of the kind of emotions that get women labeled as unstable emotionally. This stereotype may be part of the cause behind women being a small overall percentage of the highest level of professional positions. It is quite true that men are less overtly emotional than women are. It is also true that women will sometimes have a fit of emotion over domestic issues, frustration with their lives, and general dissatisfaction with clients and work. Women will often see matters as personal issues that belong solely to them and that only they can fix. Men do not feel this same level of responsibility.

So even though the normal belief in society is that women should put on a mask and push back their emotions, this is not really the best option for women in the workplace. Having an emotional reaction is nothing more than a sign that a meaningful event is taking place. It is impossible to have a place of business that is totally free of emotions. The best way to proceed is to recognize that emotions will happen and that they can be managed and used to further the employee and the business. Having the ability to tell the difference between professionalism, fact, and emotion will create strong employees in a well-functioning place of business. It is only when situations that are emotional are not handled well that the emotions of a woman can be seen as negative. The key is not to become completely emotionless by hiding all of one's emotions behind a mask. Women who give off an aura of stiffness and coldness are viewed negatively because women are supposed to be empathetic, sensitive, and caring.

Being emotional in the workplace can be an extra advantage if the person is good at managing their emotions. Contrary to being a stereotypical weakness in the place of business, the displays of emotions can easily become emotional intelligence, and that is one crucial component of the success of a business. One example of this is the speed with which women see unhappiness in their colleagues and clients. Women have the ability to see this rather quickly, and they are able to react to the situation at hand and take immediate steps to correct it. As men are seen as being more oriented toward completing tasks and less oriented toward team building, women are often put in charge of team building exercises and creating and building networks among employees.

Women will usually interact with people much better than men because they express more empathy and compassion than men do. This is part of the reason why there are more women leaders in the areas of Customer Relationships and Human Resources. The stereotype of women being creatures of emotion does not always work against them because women are excellent at building relationships, and this is an asset in the world of work. At work, it is important to build relationships that will be vital for making sure the work is completed. Winning other people over to their own point of view is something that women do well since they are inherently more sensitive and caring. Women are concerned with touching people's hearts before their minds.

This means that the idea that all emotions are illogical and disruptive and should be banned from the workplace is a notion that needs to be discarded. At the same time women need to understand that emotions are to be used and controlled, not allowed to run rampant. One example of this is the way women view issues at work. Women become personally involved, dwelling on their feelings, and overthinking the matter. This does not serve to mitigate the problem but can make it much worse. Instead, women need to step back briefly and see what steps need to be taken to handle the situation, much like a man would do. When a decision is reached, the woman can then take the necessary steps with kindness and compassion. Since virtually every decision made is affected by a woman's personal feeling, it is best if women put their focus on the long term outcome of a particular situation and the short term advantage of controlling their emotions in favor of clear thoughts.

Passion is fed by emotions, and this passion can be used by women to create successful outcomes that will bring about a sense of pride in their personal accomplishments. The one issue that often gets women in hot water is the inability to control emotions that are viewed as negative emotions like out of control bursts of anger or crying. These emotions will tend to stall a woman's career because they are seen as the disadvantage of being a woman at work. Most women will cry at one time or another. Because of this, they need to realize that some emotions will be seen as weakness and vulnerability and should not be displayed at work but should be saved for moments that are more private. A woman might need to take a moment to step away and reconsider the situation.

Businesses will not succeed in the long run if they are more focused on being robotic and macho. Many good feelings can come from emotions if businesses know how to foster the right reactions from their employees. The whole organization will be better for encouraging positive emotions. When women learn to practice emotional intelligence, they will be able to enjoy good stable relationships and rapid growth in their careers. Gaining emotional intelligence takes work and dedication, but it brings so many rewards the struggle is well worth it. Emotional intelligence is the product of five areas of self-discipline that include being aware of oneself, being able to regulate one's emotions, the motivation to achieve desired goals, a sense of empathy for others, and social skills developed enough to build networks at work and manage relationships with others.

Being aware of one's self or self-awareness can be characterized in several different ways. Self-awareness is the behavior that gives one the ability to pinpoint those minor changes in their own emotional state that are seen in physical changes such as body language, tone of voice, mood, and volume of voice. Being able to recognize these changes allows the person to work to regulate their reactions to their own emotions and to control the effects their emotions have on other people. It is worthwhile to take a few minutes every day to consider the people who populate your world and consider how you will control your emotions if an issue arises with one of them. Everyday life is very busy, and people tend to get caught up in its details and not take time to consider our coworkers and their reactions, but it can make the difference between good self-awareness and being totally unaware of how your emotions affect other people.

Being able to regulate one's own emotions, the act of self-regulation is the act of becoming aware of the factors that make up one's own emotional state. It is a necessary part of emotional intelligence because it gives the ability to improve one's emotional performance in social skills. It all comes down to developing the ability to think first before you speak. Once you become aware of your emotions, you need to be able to act consciously on your awareness to control your reactions to your emotions. This is especially important in times of high pressure or high stress. The subtle cues of physical changes in your body language will often give away what you are thinking and how your emotions are running. You need to pay careful attention to your tone of voice, eye contact, body language, and the volume of your voice. These are easy to overlook, but they often tell the true story of what you are thinking.

The motivation to achieve your desired goals come from an inner passion to better yourself. Motivation is the passion that supersedes status or money. It is vital in being able to improve your status and importance in social situations and in your career with both long term and short term goals. Motivation will help you keep sight of the goals you have set for yourself. This is a vitally important part of being a good leader. You will also need to have the motivation to keep the team's goals and the company's goal in mind and the ability to work towards all these different goals at the same time. Not only that but a good leader will assist the team in keeping sight of the goals. You will need to maintain a high level of awareness that will help drive you to realize the goals of all concerned. This type of motivation can take many different forms, and it is one of the most important parts of gaining emotional intelligence.

Empathy is a difficult concept for many people to grasp. Empathy involves having the ability to understand the emotional state of another person and to react in the proper way to that person. The connection between emotional intelligence and empathy is very close and should always be used to benefit other people and the organization as a whole. In the workplace, there are many factors that will affect overall performance—from each person's unique personal life events to availability of outside resources, from the needs of a particular client to employees struggling with the desire to perform certain tasks and listen to authority. An emotionally intelligent woman will be able to use empathy to build an environment where collaboration and understanding are daily routines used to drive the success of the business.

Social skills are vital to possess in order to have emotional intelligence. Especially in organizations that are highly service-oriented, it is necessary to possess great social skills. This will give you the ability to network effectively with others and to go beyond your emotional comfort zone when needed. Having good social skills will also give you the ability to work with many different types of people who you might encounter in your everyday work life. Remember that any time you meet someone new, you have the opportunity to open a new door that was not there before.

Emotional intelligence allows people to connect with other people, have a better understanding of their own emotions, and live happier, healthier lives. So it is extremely important to remember the five components of emotional intelligence, which are social skills, empathy, motivation, self-regulation, and self-awareness, and the four dimensions of emotional intelligence that include managing emotions, understanding emotions, using emotions to create thoughts, and perceiving emotions.

People either have a high level of emotional intelligence or a low level of emotional intelligence. There are certain characteristics that good leaders with a high level of emotional intelligence will exhibit. They are generally happy, grateful, and gracious people because their lives are going according to their own plans. They love to explore the possibilities that work and life has to offer, and they are always open-minded and curious. They are able to keep a balance between having a healthy work life and a healthy home life. Their goal is to guide a quality team to produce a quality product, but they will also be the first to admit that perfection is an impossible goal. They relate to other people easily and use empathy to understand the issues other people might be facing. They are very aware of their own selves. They freely acknowledge their own personal talents while admitting what things they need to work on. They are also well aware of what type of environment suits them best. And they know that change is a part of life and they are not afraid to change things when it is necessary to be able to grow and develop.

Those who have a low level of emotional intelligence also give off a particular set of signs that are easy to recognize if you just pay a little bit of attention to them in everyday life. Their emotions are often not appropriate for the situation. They lack empathy for others and find emotions in other people to be trivial and unnecessary. They have great difficulty in controlling their own emotions. Anything emotional, whether it is a scene from real life or a scene from a movie, has absolutely no effect on them. And they have great difficulty acquiring and maintaining personal and social relationships.

Developing emotional intelligence skills is very important to overall success. If you are able to gain an understanding of your own emotions, then you will be able to understand exactly what will lead you to success. Humans are highly social and emotional creatures. Since we already possess the skills needed, it is just a matter of gaining control over them.

Enjoying a higher level of emotional intelligence will assist you in improving your personal communication skills, becoming more resilient, boost your work performance, and help you develop good connections with other people. You will be successful in every area of life if you are able to develop a high level of emotional intelligence.

Relationship management and self-management are two very important skills to have in life. The people who possess these skills will be able to cope with life and work on even the most stressful days. You will be able to build good relationships with others while managing your own emotions in a positive manner. You will be able to speak honestly and openly with other people without offending them. You will also be able to communicate well in any type of situation. Building a high level of emotional intelligence will help you develop both of these skills.

People with a high level of emotional intelligence will easily see, identify, and resolve misunderstandings with other people. They can build trust with others because they operate with a heightened sense of trust in others. They show great empathy to other people. And they have no problem acknowledging and considering their own feelings and the feelings of other people.

Developing a high level of emotional intelligence will let you pick yourself up when you fall. It will give you the strength to go on when the way seems too long or too difficult. It will allow you to make connections with other people that are meaningful and long-lasting. It will practically guarantee your success in work and in life.

Chapter 4: Emotional Intelligence And Women In Leadership

Leadership skills are used in many different areas in the world of everyday life. They are used in politics, volunteer organizations, classrooms, schools, the workplace, and even within the family unit. Someone will always need to take charge of any given situation. People who are able to see the big picture, can take charge, set meaningful goals and create plans to reach them, and ultimately achieve what they started out to do are considered by others to be good leaders. Good leaders use their skills when working with the team, and the team will hopefully thrive under good leadership.

There are other skills that good leaders need to possess besides professional skills. It is possible to be expertly proficient in one field and highly skilled at what you do and not have the skills needed to work well with your team and to lead a team to success. This is where you need to develop your emotional intelligence. This is where you need the skills that will enable you to accurately recognize others' emotions as well as your own, know the emotional signals that other people are giving you, and be able to manage the emotions of other people as well as yourself.

Since circumstances present in the workplace are constantly changing leaders, need to be able to easily adapt to a shift in priorities. They will also need the ability to communicate these changes to their teams and to field any possible frustration and resentment the team may show because of these changes. Not everyone is as easily adaptable, and leaders need to be aware of this and have a plan in place to address this resistance. Emotional intelligence will assist an individual in being more flexible during changes in the workplace and will help you to be able to navigate through those changes with your team and not lose sight of your goals.

The best leaders, those who are most effective in their positions, all possess a high level of emotional intelligence. Technical skills and book smarts are important because they will get you to the leadership position you want to achieve. But to remain there and be effective in that role you must have a high level of emotional intelligence. Skills are nothing more than entry level keys that open the door to the executive office. Without emotional intelligence, even the best leader with the most analytical mind and the never-ending supply of great ideas will not be a good leader.

Emotional intelligence, by itself, will not get you very far. You still need to develop the skills needed to actually do the job. But taking a role in leadership and possessing a higher level of emotional intelligence will make you more successful and more effective in your position. And being adaptable is a key part of emotional intelligence because adaptability is mandatory to be a good leader. Executives and managers are held responsible for their goals, the bottom line that businesses look at daily. The most successful leaders possess most or all of the traits that are key to successful leadership and are directly related to emotional intelligence.

The skills of the leaders

Successful leaders will definitely possess and exhibit these skills:

- They will show their team members that each one is valuable to them by building relationships with them as individuals. They will show their team members that they as individuals are important to the team, their concerns are important, and their concerns will be addressed whenever possible.

- They will conduct themselves with a heightened sense of integrity and honesty, which will build their team member's trust in them.

- They will create a better working experience for their team members by focusing on teamwork and collaboration to encourage synergy among the team.

- They will constantly strive to motivate and inspire the team members through their words and actions.

- They will encourage all team members to grow and develop their individual skill level. They will always celebrate individual successes because their goal is to support and develop the team members and the team as a whole.

- They will always act with honesty and integrity with their team and with others in the organization. They will be known as someone who "walks the talk."

Employee satisfaction will rise steadily under the development of a leader who possesses emotional intelligence. Good leaders are happy in their positions and committed to their jobs, and they convey that to their team. Good leaders know how to use the power behind emotions to make individual connections with their team members, thus creating a more solidified team.

The power behind emotions to make individual connections with their team members

They do this in several ways:

- Every statement of negative feedback is preceded by at least three statements of positive feedback. For example, a good leader would say "I admire your hard work on our last project, the way you stayed late to make sure there were no loose ends, and how you helped the other team members. Today, I want to talk about your frequent absences from your desk and how that is affecting your productivity." Always begin with the positive first.

- Be curious about the employee's desire for upward mobility and do what you can to help them achieve advancement in their career. You might not want to lose a valuable team member, but you can't hold people back either.

- Look for successful events and celebrate them. A huge formal celebration is not needed but ask how little Billy's soccer game was and be genuinely happy when they win. This shows the employee that they are important to you on an individual level and not just for their contributions to the team.

- While it is important to solve problems, it is more important to put your focus on possibilities and opportunities. Many times this approach will prevent problems from arising because all problems begin as an event or an issue that is not quite right at the time. If an employee comes in late once or twice, that is an opportunity to correct a performance issue. If it is not addressed and the employee comes in late every day, they may have gotten the idea that there are above the rules of attendance that govern the team and now it has become a problem.

Some people do not realize is that a good leader with strong emotional intelligence can actually contribute to the profit level and the success of the company as a whole. A good leader is an effective leader who can lead their team to greater successes, and that leads to better performance and better overall company success.

Developing emotional intelligence is easy to do, and then again, it is not. It requires work on your part and total honesty with yourself, but if you think it is worth the work, then it will be a relatively easy thing to do. You just need to be prepared to open your mind and your soul for full viewing and be ready to accept where you are now so that you can build on your personal values to create a better you. When you are able to do this, you will have achieved emotional intelligence. You will be able to realize exactly what you are feeling, know what your emotions mean in this particular situation, and understand exactly the way your personal emotions will affect other people.

In building emotional intelligence, you will need to work on each step one at a time so that you do not miss any one component of what it takes to have emotional intelligence. To begin with, you must be self-aware. You must have an awareness of yourself and what goes on inside of you. The person who is truly self-aware will always know how they feel at any particular time, they will understand how their actions, and they know that their emotions will affect the people around them. Self-awareness in a leadership position will mean that you have a distinct picture of your personal weaknesses and strengths and that you know how to behave with honesty and humility.

There are ways to improve your level of self-awareness. It is a good idea to keep a journal and write something in it every day. Keeping a journal will assist you in developing your level of self-awareness. Just spending a few minutes each day going over your thoughts will give you the opportunity to look at them individually and take some time to think about what motivated you to act the way you did. And take the time to slow down when you need to. When you feel yourself at the beginning of a strong emotion like anger, stop and ask yourself what is going on. The situation may not be one of your own making, but you are totally in control of how you react to the situation.

Emotionally intelligent leaders will regulate themselves and their emotions in many different types of situations. These leaders will usually not attack others verbally, make decisions that are emotional or rushed, compromise their own values, or spend time stereotyping people. You gain the ability to stay in control of the situation when you are able to self-regulate. You will also be totally committed to the idea of being accountable personally, and you will know how to be flexible when needed.

There are several components to being able to self-regulate. The first step is in knowing your own personal values. You need to know exactly where you draw the line. At what point will you refuse to compromise your personal beliefs and values. Everyone has that point that they will not cross the line and you need to be very clear on what yours is. It is important to know yourself completely so that you can regulate yourself and your emotions. You need to know what values are the most important to you personally. By knowing and understanding this from the beginning, it will be easy for you to navigate troubling times and intense issues. You will automatically make the correct choice because you already know your core values and you will not need to rethink your decision.

An important part of self-regulation is the ability to accept your mistakes and hold yourself accountable for your faults. Everyone has them. But if you constantly place the blame on other people instead of admitting your own contribution to the fault, then you will need to stop immediately. You will need to be committed to being able to admit your mistakes and to having the ability to fully accept all consequences of your actions. This will earn you the respect of the people who surround you because they will see that you do not feel that you are above reproach.

Perhaps most importantly, you will need to work on remaining calm in all situations. Be aware of how you act the next time that you face a challenging situation. If you indulge in the stress relievers of crying or shouting, you need to stop those now. Those behaviors will ruin your credibility and show your lack of emotional intelligence. Learn to calm yourself by stepping away for a moment and taking deep breaths. A good exercise for dealing with these negative emotions in a positive way is to write them down on paper as exactly what you want to say while you are in this mood. Examine your words to see what you might have said so that you can determine, in private, whether or not your reaction is fair and warranted. Then think of those words and put them in a calmer tone with less threatening words. When you have calmly reviewed your reaction and mentally created a better one, tear the paper up and throw it away.

Leaders who are good at self-regulation are highly motivated leaders who know how to drive themselves and their teams to achieve their goals. They also have very high standards for the work they and their team do, and they expect a high-quality output. In times of stress, it might be easy to forget exactly why you originally wanted to take this job, so it is important to keep sight of the big picture and keep refreshing your goals as needed. Chasing the same goals all of the time make the workplace stale and irrelevant. Remain optimistic to your coworkers no matter what the current issue is. Whenever the team faces failure or even just a new challenge, take a few minutes to look for the positive elements of the situation. Every event has at least one good thing about it. It may be nothing more than the chance to meet a new person or learn a new skill, but every new challenge brings new opportunities.

A critical element to having emotional intelligence is the ability to display empathy in the workplace. Leaders who possess great empathic skills are easily able to understand how others feel in any situation. Good leaders will listen to team members when needed, they will give feedback in a constructive manner, they will be happy to provide career development to the members of their teams, and they will not be afraid to confront team members who are acting unfairly to other team members.

It is easy to improve the level of empathy you posses with a few steps. Be prepared to put yourself in the other person's shoes. It is very easy to support your own position because it is yours and you understand it. But you need to be able to use the perspective of the other person and see the situation through their point of view. Your own body language is something you should pay close attention to. Body language tells people how you really feel about the situation, even if you appear to be listening intently. Biting your lip might tell the other person that you are not comfortable in this situation. Moving your feet back and forth may give the other person the idea that you are trying to get away from the situation as soon as possible. And crossing your arms might give off the signal that you are bored or angry when it might just be that you don't know what else to do with your arms! It is all about perception and how the other person sees what you are doing. If you learn to read body language and work to keep yours always looking positive, then you will be at a great advantage. The employee's tone of voice might give them away. They might agree to work late, but you might hear the soft sigh or the hint of resignation or disappointment. Always let your teams know how much their contribution means to you and never take them for granted.

Good leaders possess good social skills. Good leaders who have emotional intelligence are good at communication, and this is one of the most important social skills a leader can possess. Good leaders will accept bad news with the same grace that they receive good news. They excel in knowing ways to get their team motivated and excited about their work. These leaders are also adept in resolving conflicts and managing changes smoothly and diplomatically. They will set the example by modeling their own behavior and will not just set back and let everyone else do all of the work. They will not leave tasks unfinished for long, and they will not compromise their personal values.

It may be necessary to practice your skills in conflict resolution. You don't need to become a professional mediator, but you do need to be able to get two people with vastly different viewpoints to find common ground to work on. Work on communicating with others and doing it well. And never think that just doing a good job is enough motivation for your team to keep doing a good job. We all like a little praise and recognition from time to time. Never hesitate to let your team members know that you value their contributions and their commitment to the team.

Perhaps the most difficult part of becoming emotionally intelligent is in developing self-control. This does not mean just knowing when to keep your mouth closed, although that is part of it. There are many different components to developing self-control, and they are all important in developing and maintaining emotional intelligence.

Think of self-control as being a specific pattern of behavior. Having physical independence, both tomorrow and today is a very real concept that we can all appreciate. What many people struggle with is that what you do today directly affects what might happen to you tomorrow. Obviously, if you rob a bank today, you will probably go to jail tomorrow (think of tomorrow as the upcoming future and not just the next day). But many people, especially those with a less developed sense of maturity, do not realize that the actions of today might reap the consequences of tomorrow. A comment you make today about a coworker might seem innocent enough, but by the time it gets to the coworker's ears, it could have been blown up to become a major verbal attack against that person. Having self-control is a matter of choosing to act according to a certain pattern of behavior rather than resorting to individual acts of behavior that may or may not be appropriate for all situations. For example, if you smoke and you stop smoking, you have chosen a particular pattern of behavior. If you choose to smoke just one cigarette, you have committed an individual act that has interrupted the pattern of behavior you are trying to establish—not smoking being the pattern of behavior. Each day you refuse to smoke makes it easier to not smoke the next day and creates a pattern of behavior.

People with self-control are very attuned to the mindsets of how and why. Questions that begin with "how" keep the mind in the present and give the opportunity to decide whether the goal is feasible or attainable. Questions that begin with "why" encourage the mind to consider the long term effects of pursuing a particular goal and whether or not that goal is as desirable as it looks right now. Distance can sometimes interfere with our ability to see the particular details of our choices. Think about wanting to be in better physical shape. The "why" is so that you can feel better and look better. The problem is in the "how" that you will use to achieve that goal. Deciding on the "how" details are an important part of the matter.

It is important when developing self-control to have the willpower to avoid temptation. Having willpower is having the psychological energy or strength to resist the temptations that might get in the way of achieving desired goals. To be able to avoid temptation, you must be able to anticipate certain situations where unwelcome desires might appear and know in advance how you will handle them. You might be able to resist chocolate cake at home, but can you resist it at the coffee shop where you stop every morning? Resisting that cake while staring right at it is called willpower. Both of these skills are crucial to have if you desire to develop emotional intelligence.

The ability to know what one's future goal is and the certainty that one will achieve that goal is confidence. People who see change as impossible to navigate will never build up any self-confidence. People who lack self-confidence will usually doubt their own abilities even if they know they are capable of succeeding and will often fail in difficult situations. People who are strongly self-confident will continue in their quest to master a goal even if the path to that goal becomes difficult to navigate.

People who truly desire to reach a particular goal usually have the motivation needed to reach that goal. A person's commitment to a goal depends a lot on how valuable that goal is to them and how likely that value is to really exist. More value in a goal brings a greater sense of motivation. Goals that have a low value or no value at all will probably not instill much motivation in a person. If you decide to lose fifty pounds so that you can look better in a swimsuit, you might not have much motivation because the cheeseburger will always taste good to you. If you decide to lose fifty pounds to save your life, you will probably be highly motivated.

When you track your progress toward a goal, you give yourself feedback so that you will know what your progress level is. This is known as self-monitoring. When you monitor or keep track, of your progress toward achieving your goal, then you are more likely to plan more activities that are related toward getting that goal. We become experts on our own behavior when we monitor ourselves, and this makes changing our habits so much easier.

Having emotional intelligence gives a person a more positive attitude. When we see ourselves a being free people with the sole responsibility for the consequences of our actions, we have the basis of self-discipline. People who have learned to take control of their own actions are much more likely to have a positive attitude about life and its events because they feel as though they are in control of their lives. This gives them a better and more productive attitude.

Setting goals is the basic building blocks of walking a path toward achieving a goal. Setting goal guides the choices that we make in life. Specific, exact goals make more sense and are easier to achieve than vague goals. Getting healthy is a very vague goal, but setting a goal to walk for one hour three times a week in order to feel better is a goal that can be achieved easily. The best way to make a goal is to follow the rules of the SMART plan: Goals should be Specific, they should be Measurable, they must be Attainable, they should be Realistic, and they must be Time-based. And sometimes, goals become more automated, and they are then kept going for a longer period of time. An automated goal usually follows the if-then system: If I walk one hour for three days each week, then I can expect to lose weight. This theory works for other ideas as well. The idea behind automated goals is to set up a structure of recurring behavior that is reinforced by consistent rewards and goal achievement. The beauty of this is that people do not always need to keep their goals in the focus of their minds so that they will automatically revert to their good habits even during stress.

Women in the workforce have more permission to be emotionally intelligent than men do. As little girls, they are encouraged to show empathy to others, to develop meaningful and deep relationships with other people, and the use words that express feelings and emotions. Girls might develop some toughness while playing sports, just as boys do, but they are still likely to follow the more feminine mindset as they grow to adulthood. Boys growing into men generally display the skills that are considered hard like anger and aggression. Women are encouraged from birth to develop and display the soft skills that make up the definition of emotional intelligence.

Men will complain that most women are too emotional, and women will complain that most men are not emotional enough. This statement has some basis in truth. When a woman encounters someone who is upset, she will likely feel that emotion inside herself and will be able to empathize with that person. Men may feel bad for a few seconds, but then their brain switches over to the problem-solving mode, which is how little boys and little girls are programmed from birth to behave. Both methods have their place in emotional intelligence. Using the male method of tuning out upsetting emotions is helpful when it is necessary to remove yourself from the distress so that you can make a decision or so that you can take charge when other people are falling apart everywhere. Women will stay with the emotion long enough to support and nurture other people in times of distress. It has always been believed that women can learn the strength traits of men but that men cannot learn to be nurturing like women are.

It isn't that men can't learn empathy; it is a case of men being expected to be strong and macho and not show their softer sides. That may all change one day, but for now, women have the upper hand in the emotional intelligence department. Women are better at gauging the emotions in a room within seconds of walking in. Women are much better than men at seeing events from the viewpoint of the other person. And women excel at being able to pinpoint the source of the bull in any situation. Women need to remember that the important point is not to learn to act like a man but to use femininity along with personal strengths to lead others.

Always keep in mind that good leaders follow three basic rules that are mandatory for anyone who desires to become a good leader.

Never worry about having to settle discipline on your subordinates when needed. Do not worry about whether or not your employees like you because it does not matter. The ones you want to keep might feel slighted for a bit, but they will realize that the discipline was necessary and they will want to stay with you because you are a good boss. The ones who quit probably needed to go away anyway.

You are who you are, and no one else. You are not the King of England or the leader of the free world, and you cannot expect to run your life or your job the same way they do. It is quite alright to take good ideas from other leaders but remembers, in the end, you are you, and there will never be anyone else who will ever be you.

Do not take workplace events personally, even if it is tempting to do so. Of course, women are sensitive to emotions, more so than men are, but it is never a good idea to let emotions control your thinking or getting between you and a logical solution. Emotional intelligence is all about feeling emotions AND having the strength to make sometimes unpleasant decisions.

In the workplace, it is highly reasonable to think that women have the innate ability to become quite successful by using their own emotional intelligence to get ahead in the world. Emotional intelligence is the key to success for women and should be embraced and developed by all women.

Chapter 5: Self-Confidence

Self-confidence is one of the indicators of emotional intelligence. Having a balanced and positive attitude has much to do with having good self-confidence. Having the knowledge that you can do what needs to be done is the basis of self-confidence. Obstacles do not stop a person who has good self-confidence. People who are self-confident will not only overcome obstacles, but they will also be able to accept the credit for a job done well. Every small success that is won is a building block for even larger successes.

Almost every element that is involved in a full and happy life requires self-confidence. Developing more confidence will help you to quiet the little voice inside that keeps you from having the ability to do the things you want to do. It will also give you several other benefits you may not have thought of before.

Women who are self-confident are less likely to suffer from anxiety and fear. You will be better able to dismiss the thoughts that might keep you from acting in the way that your personal values tell you that you should be acting. Women who suffer from low self-confidence are well aware of the tendency to constantly overthink perceived mistakes and agonizing worries, replaying them in your mind over and over. In building your self-confidence, you will then be able to quiet that annoying internal critic, and you will be able to stop overthinking every little conceived mistake.

Those who have a greater sense of self-worth from self-confidence are less focused on themselves and are abler to build good relationships with other people. Most people are so involved in their own worries and thoughts that they are not able to climb out of their own heads and create good relationships with others. And you will find more enjoyment in these moments of interaction because you will not be concerned with the type of impression you are making on others. You just won't care about it. And you will be so relaxed with your new self-confidence that you will easily make deeper connections with new people you meet.

Self-confidence helps you to cope with failure by giving you the skills you need to overcome any setback that life puts in your path. This is not to say that you will never fail. But when you do fail to achieve a goal, you will not be devastated by the loss, but you will be able to go on with strength. As you become stronger in your confidence, you will look at these instances less as failures and more as opportunities to learn how to overcome challenges. And those who do not fear failure actually succeed more often because they are not waiting for every circumstance to be completely perfect before they act. They know that nothing is ever one hundred percent perfect.

Working to build self-confidence will give you greater personal motivation through improving your sense of personal accomplishment. Anytime you learn or conquer a new skill; you learn ways to succeed that serve to increase your desire to succeed more. Success drives motivation.

Your real self becomes more apparent when you are a self-confident woman. You will be abler to accept the weaknesses that you own because you will realize that they do not diminish your personal self-worth. You will also be better able to use your strengths more completely and more fully than ever before. You will enjoy a greater sense of purpose because you will now act in the way that your values say you should act. You will have the ability to speak up, show up, and stand up for what you think is the right way to act. Your best self ever will definitely shine through.

So why do so many women lack the self-confidence necessary to break through barriers in the workplace and achieve the success that men have known for so long? Women still fail to achieve all but a very few of the top positions in companies. Women as a group face several structural barriers that hinder them economically and socially. Those barriers include the lack of affordable child care, the fact that women are usually employed in areas where job security is low or non-existent, the lowering of the value of jobs traditionally held by women, and the gap in wages between men and women.

These barriers mean that fewer women are currently holding top-level positions in most companies. It is mostly these external factors that cause barriers to women moving up in the workplace world, and this fact alone can cause a great lack of self-confidence in women. These barriers mean that women are far less likely than men to speak up for their own advancement even if they know that their supervisor will not support their career choices. Women usually take far fewer risks than men do because they do not feel supported by their peers at work. Women do not normally feel comfortable in speaking their minds at work. And since women are more likely to be kept indefinitely in lower level positions, they are less likely to develop the self-confidence they need to succeed. Because of this, they are more likely to feel unmotivated and uninspired by the work they do.

Oftentimes women are held back by institutional mindsets. These include stereotypes and gender biases. People have long held the belief that men and women do better in different types of jobs. Men have long been thought to be superior in jobs that require physical strength and strong character. Women have been thought to be better suited to the roles that come from caring and nurturing. And many people associate men with the traits that have long been thought to be necessary for top-level management positions—self-reliance, independence, dominance, competitiveness, aggression, and assertiveness. When women do reach top-level positions, they are expected to act both like women and like men. Women in leadership positions must walk on a very fine line between two very opposite sets of expectations.

Women are often restrained by their own individual mindsets. These are behaviors and thoughts that women sometimes have that can hold them back from success. Most women do not pursue the small percentage of jobs in the upper echelon of the company because they want to avoid office politics, they prefer a balance to work and life, they have an aversion to taking risks, they bow to the pressures of society, or they simply lack the self-confidence to apply for the jobs. This means that few women are currently in the position of vice president or president.

Because of the fact that women often want different things than men do, they more often gravitate toward the private sector where they are able to avoid many of the barriers that women still face in large companies. Here, they have discovered fewer stereotypes about traditional female jobs and more female role models and mentors. Also, in the private sector, women are more likely to be leaders and owners, thus building their self-confidence more than they would in the public sector.

Women often feel the need to make certain choices in lifestyles that hinder their advancement in the public sector. Women often choose to start families, care for other family members, and prefer a better balance between the working life and the private life than they would likely have in the public sector. Even women who take on the role of primary breadwinner are often also the primary caregiver in the family. None of these choices are inherently bad, but they all make a contribution to the gender leadership gap.

Most women will face one or more of these barriers at some point in their lives. At times the barrier will be bold and overt, and other times the barrier will be hidden in a different agenda. People still feel that women with small children will not want certain jobs or will not do well in certain jobs because they will one day need to choose between work and home life, and the children will be the winners.

Women need to begin thinking about their overall development in the physical, intellectual, and emotional areas so that they can enjoy true career growth. They need to start challenging the idea that they must act or work a certain way just because they are women. Just because women are groomed from birth to feel emotions and be caring and nurturing does not mean that women are not well suited for the business world. On the contrary, women have an innate strength of will that can help them to be successful at anything they try to do in life. Women need to develop all of their abilities and increase their level of emotional intelligence.

Society still encourages girls and women to be more empathic and to develop meaningful, deep relationships with others. Because most people still assume that women are the tender nurturers of society, professional women are given the advantage of being more authentic and more vulnerable at work. Being more real helps women to build a certain level of trust among their employees and co-workers. Leaders who are trusted are able to build teams that are more result-driven, motivated, and successful than leaders who have trouble sharing their emotions.

Emotional intelligence is a key ingredient that can launch a career, and women are far superior to men in learning and using emotional intelligence to be successful in work and in life.

Chapter 6: Health and Wellness

People generally understand the relationship between healthy behaviors and a healthy life. They know that if you take risks with your health, then you might just make yourself sick. So people dress warmly when they go out in the cold and wash their hands when they get dirty. Many people are unaware that our emotional health can have a dramatic effect on our physical health. And there is a definite link between high levels of emotional intelligence and physical health and wellbeing.

There are three components of emotional intelligence that give you a way to measure how strong you feel our emotional intelligence level really is. You can rate your level on these components and know where your level of emotional intelligence is. It is important to be honest because only by knowing where you truly are can you ever hope to improve. These three components are attention, clarity, and repair.

In emotional intelligence, attention is the ability to pay attention to the moods and feelings of other people. In other words, it measures how well you do at feeling empathy. Paying attention to the needs of other people is a large part of feeling empathy. Feeling empathy can also be beneficial to you personally. It can relieve stress, promote better overall health, and reduce or prevent job stress and burn-out. When you can relate to the needs and feelings of another person, you build a connection with that person. True empathy requires simply listening and caring. It removes the need to fix things, advise on a course of action, or place blame. Feeling empathy for other people gives you a unique perspective and a sense of peacefulness that connects you to that other person.

People who are emotionally intelligent have had experience with a large variety and a wide range of feelings. They have felt fulfillment to the greatest heights and despair and depression to the lowest depths. This gives them the ability to relate with many more people than someone who has not either experienced these feelings or taken the time to analyze their own feelings.

When we feel empathy for another, we join their world, and we relate to them with a connection that involves both compassion and emotion. It is not necessary to completely understand someone's problem or to even agree with it to feel empathy for them. It is only necessary to be there and to be available. The problem some people have is that they can't feel empathy without letting their own judgments, opinions, and egos getting in the way. It is usually very easy to empathize with someone who you care for and agree with. It is more difficult to empathize with a stranger with a viewpoint that is radically different from yours or who is in a situation you have never faced.

But being able to feel empathy with other people in any situation is a key component to the success and health of our lives and relationships. Empathy is a major part of our own wellbeing and emotional intelligence. It is equally important to get past the emotions that can make it difficult for you to feel empathy. If you fear someone or something, it will be difficult to truly feel compassion and empathy for that person or situation. Being judgmental can cause you to put up a mental roadblock against someone who truly needs your empathy. And fear of a person or situation will likely prevent you from showing empathy.

In order to truly feel empathy for others, which will, in turn, raise your level of emotional intelligence and improve your overall health, it is important to do three things. You need to be able to be honest about your own feelings, you will need to truly feel what the other person is feeling, and you must learn to forgive others and yourself. All of these three traits will not only make you more emotionally intelligent but will also make you healthier.

When you can be honest about your feelings, you are acknowledging that you have feelings, and you are not afraid to express them. This ability will truly remove much of the judgment and negativity from your life and will make you feel truly liberated. You will no longer need to hide the inner truth that makes up you. Whenever feelings of defensiveness and judgment with another person rise up, admit to your own times of feeling these emotions. Feel free to own, admit to, and freely express your own feelings of insecurity, sadness, anger, and fear. Keeping these emotions bottled up inside is not good for your mental health or your physical health. Mental health issues can cause physical symptoms so by relieving your mind of its burdens, you will also relieve your body of all the aches and pains it has been holding inside.

It is sometimes difficult to understand the feelings of another person if you have never felt that feeling or been in that situation. But being able to imagine the pain they are feeling is vital to feeling empathy for them. You must be able to put yourself into the shoes of someone else. This will give you the ability to use your imagination to feel what they are feeling. Imagination is a wonderful thing that children use in great abundance. Somehow as adults, people stop imagining, but creativity is a necessity for emotional intelligence. It will never hurt to try being creative, especially if you remember that creativity is a personal thing and do not judge your level of creative against someone else.

An important part of mental healing is the ability to forgive others as well as forgive you. No one is perfect in this world. Holding onto past issues creates a feeling of pain and negativity inside and will not lead you to a peaceful, fulfilling life. Begin by forgiving yourself all the little faults you have— real or imagined. Being able to forgive yourself will release all the self-judgment you hold inside and can give you a new perspective on your life. When you are able to forgive yourself truly, you will be better able to forgive others. And forgiveness will remove a great mental weight that keeps your thoughts low and depressed.

Another important part of emotional intelligence is emotional clarity, which is the ability to clearly discriminate between our own feelings. Clarity is also important to feel empathy because it is impossible to truly feel your emotions if you do not understand them. But by being able to know and understand your own emotions, you will be better able to know why you are feeling those emotions. People who have poor emotional clarity will not be able to know and understand where their emotions are coming from.

If you can develop an understanding of the origins of your emotions, you are able to take actions that will change the thoughts or the circumstances that caused those emotions. It is when you do not understand where an emotion came from that you are not able to address it and get rid of it. And if you are not sure exactly what emotions you are feeling, it will be impossible to regulate your emotions. It is relatively easy to develop the emotional clarity that will enhance your emotional intelligence and improve your health and wellbeing.

Learn to give your emotions plain names and call them by their plain names. In today's society, it is not popular to speak about personal feelings in most public settings. You use words that everyone can relate to, but that does not really mean what you are trying to say. You use words like "stoked" or "stressed" that other people understand but that are not really words that describe emotions.

But people have become accustomed to using metaphors instead of saying how they really feel. They refuse to use words that may sound childish to describe their emotions. But there is nothing wrong with the words happy, sad, excited, fearful, or nervous. If you are not able to clearly talk about the way you are feeling, it will be difficult or nearly impossible to think how you are feeling clearly. Before you are able to make sense of and navigate how you really feel, it is important to be able to talk about you are feeling in plain language.

In learning to express emotions in plain language, it is also a good exercise to imagine all the possible synonyms that could go with a particular emotion. If you are feeling anger, are you also feeling annoyance, frustration, rage, and irritability? When you feel fear do you also feel shocked, fright, terror, panic, or anxiety? The more that you are fluent with using real emotional language, the better and more clearly you will be able to think about how you are feeling and to express how you are feeling.

Once you are able to give real names to your emotions, you can begin to separate the emotion from the physical feeling. If stress is making you feel tense, ask yourself if the tense you are feeling is an emotion or a physical feeling. You might say it is both and you would probably be right. If a situation makes you feel tense, your body begins to feel tension by tightening up muscles and putting nerves on high alert. This syndrome is part of the natural fight or flight syndrome that helps to protect us in times of danger. While this feeling has its place, it is not needed as often as our body might feel it. When you feel fear, your body tightens up and makes more adrenalin to fuel your escape. By acknowledging fear and feeling tense, you are able to lessen its effects or eliminate it altogether. Then your muscles and nerves won't react quite as violently and your body will not put out the rush of adrenaline that it does not need. This will help to lower the overall stress that you feel physically and will help your body maintain a more neutral feeling. This will help lower you blood pressure and may result is fewer headaches and other stress-related reactions.

And part of learning emotional clarity is having the ability to not only name your emotions but also to validate them. While we like to fix situations and solve problems, not everything in life needs fixing, and emotions are one of these things. Sometimes, emotions just need to be what they are—emotions.

They might make you feel bad, but they are not bad in themselves. They just are. Emotions by themselves are not problems. They can cause problems if you let them. So instead of dedicating time to fixing your emotions all the time, sometimes it is best to just label them for what they are, accept their presence, and get on with your life.

Once you have learned to admit to your emotions and developed the ability to name and accept your emotions, then it is time to repair your emotions. This refers to the ability to create some form of regulation with your moods. Moods are funny things. They can pop up when you least expect it. Sometimes, you are not even certain at first what caused the mood, and you find yourself diving in to find the root cause. This is a good thing because it takes you to the heart of the matter so that you can begin to fix the mood.

Having the ability to regulate your emotions will give you the ability to regulate your moods. Emotions are good, but they have their time and their place. Laughing at something funny on your phone during lunch at an outdoor café is appropriate and harmless. Laughing at something funny on your phone during a business meeting when the CEO is giving the financial report is probably not a good idea. Laughing by itself is not bad; on the contrary, it is very healthy for people to laugh. Laughing at the wrong time or in the wrong place is not good.

Many emotional responses do not need any form of self-regulation. If that emotion is relevant to the situation and you feel better when you do it, by all means, enjoy it. This means that if the situation is correct, feel free to laugh, cry, show anger, or be sad. Doing so can also put you in a place to create a relationship with someone else, even if it is brief and ends there. Laughing with others at a funny movie temporarily creates a relationship between the people in the theater. Later, everyone will go a different way, but for now, they are part of a group.

The inability to regulate personal emotions and moods is the mark of personality disorders, depression, social anxiety, and behavioral issues. Being able to control your moods will help you advance socially. This does not mean to ignore them when they happen. This is truly controlling the mood, admitting to its existence but refusing to allow it to take over your entire life. By using a few simple steps, you will soon be able to regulate your moods easily.

The first step is in knowing when you need to make the situation fit your needs. Try to avoid those situations that you know will make you feel emotions that you don't want to feel. If heavy traffic makes you angry, then try to leave the house a bit earlier, so maybe the traffic will be lighter. If standing in the fast food line for lunch makes you impatient, you could bring your lunch from home and have your whole lunch period for eating and relaxing. The key is in knowing what situations give you certain moods and rearranging what you do to hopefully avoid those situations.

If you are not able to completely change the situation, then you might be able to change certain parts of it in order to control your moods. Perhaps you love to entertain, but you get so depressed because you can't manage a five-course dinner for 12 with rich wines and fine china. Maybe you can change certain aspects of that situation, in order to better suit your talents. Make the next dinner party a themed buffet on fancy designer paper plates with a marvelous punch type drink for thirst quenching. You might not be able to make duck a l'orange, but you can probably manage seasoned taco meat or trays of sliced deli meats. Your guests will probably have a better time, too. You have removed a stressor from your life and controlled a mood all at once.

You can also shift the focus of your attention. You know you need to go to the gym to work out so that you can become a healthier person but look at all those gym regulars who strut the hard body that you don't currently have just makes you feel defeated. You have now created a mood. But remember, they did not grow up looking like that. Put your focus and attention back on you and what you want to accomplish. Never judge your progress by someone else's because everyone is unique and should stay that way.

And if you have tried to modify the situation, change it completely, or look the other way and none of those tactics worked for you, then it may be time to change the way you react to the situation. Gain control of the emotional response that happens when you are in certain situations. You will probably need first to get control of your immediate response. Heavy traffic on your commute to work might make your heart pound. Take deep, slow breaths and thing calm thoughts. The traffic will go away eventually, either because people will get out of your way or you will arrive at work. If something strikes you funny at an inappropriate moment, try to keep your facial expression neutral. Your eyes might be glinting with laughter, but at least your expression will be appropriate. And these tactics will allow you to control your mood.

Having emotional intelligence causes you to have better health practices. Those people who are more emotionally intelligent are more likely to maintain a healthy regimen of self-care, like eating right and exercising. Those who are emotionally intelligent are also better able to cope with stressful situations in life and better able to readily adapt to unexpected changes in daily life. These are good coping strategies that bring added benefits to personal health. Some examples of healthy behavior are getting enough sleep every day, engaging in regular exercise, and consuming a healthy diet. All of these behaviors will lead to a more positive outlook on life and a better quality of life.

And the benefits of emotional intelligence do not stop there. While people with a high level of emotional intelligence are more likely to take care of themselves physically, they are also more likely to refrain from situations that would put them in the path of potential harm. They are less likely to engage in taking abusive substances and risk-taking activities.

People who are deeply in tune with their own emotions and can accept and regulate their moods are more likely to be better able to cope when they find themselves in situations of stress. They are much more likely than other people to seek medical attention when needed, to accept the normal changes that might be happening in their bodies, and to take paths in life that will lead them to better overall health. This can be seen in their avoidance of addictive substances like alcohol or nicotine. Also, these people will be more likely to engage in a regular routine of physical activity and will strive to make healthy choices for food consumption. All of these behaviors are clearly tied to a high level of emotional intelligence with an acceptance of their own personal reality and accountability for their personal physical wellbeing. The person who is aware of self and regulates their own self will possess a high level of emotional intelligence and will also live a better overall life.

Chapter 7: Relationships

Emotional intelligence is the ability to think about emotional information and emotions and to enhance your thought processes through the proper use of emotions.

Understanding our own emotions and the emotions of other people is crucial to learning to improve relationships with others. Low emotional intelligence will lead people to make inappropriate remarks to bosses or coworkers, become extremely angry over trivial matters, or make snap decisions without knowing all the facts involved and regretting the decision later.

A higher level of emotional intelligence will bring you better job performance, will help you work better on a team, will help you retain information better, will increase your personal levels of creativity and performance, and will elevate your ability to accept change. And emotionally intelligent people enjoy deeper, more intense personal relationships.

People who are emotionally intelligent are far better than others at monitoring their own activity and taking stock of their own emotions and reactions. And those who think of their partners as possessing a high level of emotional intelligence are happier in their partnerships and feel as though those relationships will continue to be happy in the future. People with a high level of emotional intelligence readily understand four distinct things:

They can read the emotions of other people. Emotionally intelligent people are able to read the emotions of people who might not be very open with their emotions.

Being able to understand and regulate their own emotions is the mark of an emotionally intelligent person. These people are in tune with their own emotions. They do not brush them aside, mislabel them, or bury them deep inside. They do know how to regulate their emotions and to hang on to a mood until it is appropriate to display that mood.

People who are emotionally intelligent know their thoughts are the creators of their emotions and that they can decrease the power of their emotions by controlling their thoughts and regulating their emotions. They also know that moods can enhance certain ways of thinking and that they function better when calm.

Those who are emotionally intelligent know there is a direct connection between the emotional reactions of other people and their own actions.

Developing emotional intelligence takes work, but it is the best way to improve your relationships with others. Whether you are trying to improve your parenting skills with your child, become a roommate who is easier to live with, or become a better partner in your relationship, gaining emotional intelligence can directly enhance your relationships for the better.

Emotional intelligence makes you better at listening. Being a good listener for others is a key component of maintaining a deep romantic relationship for a long period of time. Being tuned in with the emotional needs of your partner and understanding your own emotional needs will make you a receptive, active listener. People who are in relationships with people who are good listeners have improved emotional states and less stress psychologically.

It is likely that in most relationships nothing stays the same for very long. Personalities, homes, hairstyles, and careers all change given enough time, and emotional intelligence will give you the strength to weather these changes with minimal fuss. Emotionally intelligent people are more likely to understand that change happens and they can anticipate it better, making it easier for them to adjust to the changes and not run away from them.

Empathy is a major component in maintaining a good long term relationship. Emotionally intelligent people are masters at feeling empathy for other people, so they are more easily able to feel a partner's feelings even when they do not share the same feelings. And this feeling of empathy can also make it easier for you to anticipate those things your partner needs even if they are not spoken. When you instinctively know that your partner needs a hug or you stop to pick up their favorite ice cream for no reason, you are using empathy to show you are in touch with your partner's thoughts and feelings.

Healthy relationships are never perfect, and being able to accept a certain amount of criticism is necessary in any good relationship. This helps the relationship to grow or to change as needed. Emotionally intelligent people find it relatively easy to accept feedback from their partner when it is constructive and will help the relationship grow. And they will not feel the need to take this criticism personally or get defensive. Along with this, each partner can focus on their own priorities and feel free to be able to share them with their partner. Since it is sometimes easy to put a relationship on the back burner while putting all their effort into surviving everyday life, the emotionally intelligent person knows the need for not ignoring their relationships and will continuously put in the effort needed to keep the relationship alive and well.

Since emotionally intelligent people are more in more in touch with their own emotions, they are also more available emotionally in their relationships. It is easy for their partners to come to them when they have a need because the partner knows they will be accepted without judgment or ridicule. The emotionally intelligent person knows how to handle their own emotions, and they can handle their partner's emotions, too. Part of the emotional ease they carry themselves with is the ability not to get caught up in difficult situations but to work through them with their partner to solve them.

Partners who are emotionally intelligent can easily see the good in each other and will work to bring it out. They know when they are not giving their partner the attention they need without the partner needing to say anything. They are also easily able to see when their partner is caught up in real life and to know that their partner is not pushing them aside out of spite or neglect. They are able to give their partner a little consideration for trying and not be so concerned with their partner failing.

Emotional intelligence will make you a more committed partner. They understand that leaving a committed relationship would be a devastating proposal and they will do anything in their power to keep the love strong and the fire flaming. Emotional intelligence is the key that keeps couples firmly rooted in long term relationships that are still going strong years later.

It is easier to get the things that you want from a relationship if you possess emotional intelligence. You will be better able to ask for the things you want and need instead of assuming that your partner or roommate will automatically know what you are thinking. When you know the proper way to ask, it is more likely you will get what you want. And much of living with someone else involves personal compromise, something that people who have emotional intelligence are very good at doing. Emotionally intelligent people easily understand the perspective of the other person in the relationship, and they are able to weigh their needs against the needs of the other person and come to a reasonable solution.

One of the biggest killers in any type of relationship is the lack of respect from the other partner. Disrespectful behavior is not something anyone needs to worry about when they are in any kind of relationship with a person with emotional intelligence. This includes being able to share things and space without too much overt worry about mine and yours. Having emotional intelligence makes you realize that your partner's or roommate's needs are just as important as your own and should not be ignored or brushed aside since this is just a form of disrespect that an emotionally intelligent person would not do. You are able to see where the other person is coming from and what motivates them to act the way they do.

Those with healthy relationships with their roommates and significant others are more mindful of their own reactions and what they might mean to the other person. Emotionally intelligent and mindful partners will make choices that will benefit the relationship rather than the individual. One of these choices is the choice to be an independent person and not to be overly co-dependent on the partner in the relationship. Emotionally intelligent people know that extreme dependency leads to relationship strain, and they will avoid it.

Emotionally intelligent people have no need to engage in behavior that is passive-aggressive. Passive-aggressive behaviors involve being indirectly aggressive rather than overtly aggressive. People who engage in this behavior will resist demands or requests from their partners or roommates because they know it is annoying and offensive to their partners. Emotionally intelligent people are naturally more thoughtful because they have nothing to prove by acting badly and everything to gain by keeping things peaceful in the relationship. So emotionally intelligent people have no problem going the extra mile to do something thoughtful like tidying up the house or cooking dinner for their partner or roommate since they know the little things keep the relationship happy.

When emotionally intelligent people find themselves in the middle of a relationship conflict, they are able to solve it without blowing the whole relationship up in the process. They know that conflicts that are resolved using kindness and effective resolution techniques are less likely to cause permanent damage to the relationship. They understand the importance of keeping events civil and pleasant. One reason for this is because emotionally intelligent people are more patient with other people than might be considered normal or usual. Emotionally intelligent parents know that children are not just small sized adults and that they will do things differently from what adults will. They know to be extremely patient with their little ones as they learn the things they need to know to grow into healthy adults. Emotionally intelligent partners will automatically step back if only mentally, to take the time needed to assess the situation from an impersonal perspective so they do not end up saying or doing something that will ruin the relationship.

It is easy to assume that the partner who loves you will automatically feel the way you do about all matters that are important to you, but that simply is not true. Emotionally intelligent people will never make the mistake of projecting their own emotions onto their partner or their child. They will understand that everyone has their own way of thinking and their own thoughts. Also, they will be able to know the difference between whether or not you are letting your own emotions rule everything or if the emotions or behavior really belong to the child or partner. And because you are in tune with their emotions, you will realize when they can handle things on their own and when they really need assistance from a loving source. Sometimes, even adults have a hard time asking for help from their family and friends, but the emotionally intelligent person will know without being told.

People with high levels of emotional intelligence are naturally more confident individuals. This is especially important when dealing with children because it is sometimes necessary to not back down from your decisions. Sometimes, you will need to hold on to your decisions in the interest of raising disciplined and healthy children. And your children will recognize this because you are more open to being approached when a loved one needs help. You also have the sense to know when a loved one has the tools they need to figure matters out on their own, and you have the strength to step back and let them try it on their own.

People who are intelligent emotionally are able to have intense conversations about critical matters without fear of escalating into an argument. Instead of feeling blamed or attacked by the opinions of others, emotionally intelligent people view a healthy argument as a chance to grow by learning the other person's point of view. They gain a better understanding of the other person by listening to them.

In personal relationships, it is important to recognize the importance of emotional intelligence and the impact it will have on the relationship. Individuals who do not know their own emotions can't begin to understand their emotions or the emotions of others. The will struggle to maintain healthy relationships with others. The person with a high level of emotional intelligence will be able to handle any emotional aspect of the relationship without losing their composure or their strength of will.

Chapter 8: Developing Emotional Intelligence

So while women are inherently better at possessing emotional intelligence than men are, and even though women have been groomed from birth to have some of the traits of emotional intelligence, it is not a simple matter of understanding other people and saying you possess emotional intelligence. Having emotional intelligence is a major component of creating and growing any type of personal or professional relationship. Emotional intelligence gives you the ability to manage and understand your own emotions and those of the people around you. It is a vitally important skill to have to be able to navigate relationships with your significant other, family, friends, colleagues, and your boss.

Three primary components of emotional intelligence

There are three primary components of emotional intelligence. They are the ability to develop excellent social skills, the personal motivation to look at a problem rationally and work out a solution, and acute self-awareness. These are all things that can be worked at and developed over time so that you can boost your own sense of self-awareness. Developing this ability will help you to develop a much stronger sense of self-awareness, and that will directly impact your ability to interpret other people's emotions and to be able to respond well to them. It can also give you a reasonably good insight into your own emotions and how they affect you and others.

There are many things one needs to learn and practice to ultimately learn emotional intelligence.

Always do your best to remain connected to other people. When you are under stress, it is a natural reaction to want to withdraw from society so that no one will see your shame and embarrassment when you really need to save money, or for whatever reason, you can invent for hiding at home in your pajamas. But people are social creatures, and our happiness is directly tied to our level of social interaction. Being connected to other people is one of the key components of happiness. In order to remain socially connected continue going to church, join a support group if needed, or maybe take a class at the community center where no one knows you personally if you crave social contact but want to remain anonymous. The important thing is to stay connected with other people, so you don't spend all of your time over-analyzing yourself.

Women in the business world are operating in an environment that is mostly dominated by men. To survive in an environment that is mostly male-dominated, women tend to try to use more logic and less intuition, which is what they are better at and is a key component of emotional intelligence. Women are learning that they cannot compete in the male business world by becoming just like men. Women need to return to the skills that make them excellent leaders. Emotional intelligence can be learned, and it is never too late to begin.

Pay attention to the way you react to other people around you. Do you wait to know all the facts or do you jump to snap decisions? Do you believe in stereotypes? Pay much more attention to the way you interact with other people and how you act toward other people. Spend some time thinking about how other people might be feeling and try to be more accepting of their positions and more open with your opinions of them.

Look around at the environment where you work. Do you look for praise or attention for your personal accomplishments? Being humble is wonderful when it is necessary, but the workplace is not the place to practice humility all of the time. Your accomplishments will bring you recognition sometimes, and there are times when it will be better if you step back and let others receive the accolades. When you are humble, accept the thanks and then be confident about it quietly. Whenever possible, give the limelight to other people and give them the opportunity to shine. Let the focus be on them for a while.

Evaluate yourself and your traits. What are your strengths and your weaknesses? You need first to be able to accept the fact that you are not perfect and that you have a long way to go. Look at yourself honestly and have the courage to make the needed changes. It will change your life. Look at how you react when the situation is stressful. If you are guilty of becoming upset every time there is a delay or the situation does not do the way you want, then you have issues that need to be worked on. Do you become angry at other people or blame them for events that are not their fault? Part of the concept of being emotionally intelligent is the ability to stay in control and remain calm during difficult situations and stressful times. This is a trait that is valued very highly both in the business world and the social world.

Never be afraid to take responsibility for your own actions and do not point the finger at anyone else. Admit to your own blame in the matter and take your punishments and consequences as they come. Making sure the other person gets their punishment is not your job. If you have hurt someone's feeling, even accidentally, quickly apologize directly to the person; never try to avoid them and think the situation will go away on its own. Most people are willing to forgive you and to forget the wrong if you are contrite and honestly try to make amends. Always take the time to consider how your actions will affect other people before you commit the action. If you feel that your decision will have a negative effect on other people, then maybe you need to decide on another course of action. If it is something that you must absolutely do, then you need to ask yourself how you will be able to help other people deal with the effects of your decision to act.

Everyone has positive emotions and negative emotions, but the key is in learning how your negative emotions can best be managed to minimize their effect on others. Being able to reduce and manage those negative emotions will make you much less likely to feel overwhelmed by them. So the next time someone is doing or saying something designed to upset you, refuse to rise to the bait. Do not jump to conclusions. Step back and let yourself see the situation from a variety of different ways. Always try to look at events objectively so that they don't bother you as much. Your perspective will easily change when you are more mindful of your own emotions.

Spend some time every day working on your vocabulary so that your communication skills will improve. People who are emotionally intelligent generally use more specific phrases and words to get their meaning across to other people. When they discover they have some sort of deficiency in communication, they work to correct it as soon as possible. Whenever some situation does not go exactly to your liking, take a few minutes to think about it and try to decide exactly what you did not like. Decide what exactly made the situation so unbearable and think what you would do differently the next time. If you can name exactly what went wrong, you have a better chance of correcting the issue the next time it arises.

Watching other people's verbal and non-verbal cues will give you valuable insight into the emotions and feelings of others. Focus on other people and think about what they go through on a daily basis. Keep in mind that all people have their own issues, and even though this has no excuse, it is better met with empathy and not scorn.

Be prepared to admit to the things that cause you to stress and take steps to have less of those situations in your life. If it is a particular person who causes you problems, then avoid them. There is no rule that says you need to be nice to everyone. It might be better if you pick the people who you surround yourself with so that you can work on keeping your own emotions in check.

Do your best to bounce back when adversity knocks you down. All people encounter issues and challenges. The key to emotional intelligence is how you choose to react to the events that challenge you, the event that send you into a complete meltdown or set you on the path to success. Positive thinking will always take you a long way; there is no doubt about that. You will more easily recover from adversity when you look at situations with optimism and not with words of complaining. Always think what you can learn from a situation. See what this challenge can teach you about your inner strengths and your desire to succeed.

Observe how different situations make you feel. Everyone is busy with their hectic lifestyles, and it is too easy to stop focusing on emotions and just run on autopilot. Take the time every day to reconnect with yourself and see how you are doing. And while you are spending some time with yourself, take some time to focus on your behavior and see if anything needs correcting. When a stressful situation presents itself, pay attention to how you are feeling. Managing your emotions will be easier when you spend some time every day thinking about how they affect your everyday life.

Never fail to take responsibility for your own emotions. Your behavior and your emotions come from inside of you, not from anywhere else. When you begin to take the responsibility necessary for your own actions and emotions, you will begin to be able to correct those things in your mindset that need correcting.

Whenever you feel you are on a positive path to the goal of emotional intelligence, take a little time to celebrate your successes. One key component of possessing emotional intelligence is the ability to constantly reflect on your emotions, celebrating the positive accomplishments, and correcting the negative ones. Life is not stagnant; it changes constantly. You probably have not encountered all of the new situations you will face in your lifetime. So one does not simply gain emotional intelligence and keep it forever. Once you have it, you probably have it, but you will need to continue to keep growing in your learning and your abilities. Remember that the emotions that are positive are stronger and will give you more meaningful relationships with others. But do not ignore the negative emotions, and do not repress them either. Take them out and look at them when they happen. Negative emotions need to be reflected on and analyzed to see why they happened and how they can be changed. This is the true key to making yourself into a well-rounded individual.

Life will send many different situations your way, and there will be stress when some of these happen. Breathe deeply whenever possible to prevent the emotions you feel from becoming explosions of anger or sadness. Take some time to be alone and think about the situation. Get a grip on the situation and decide how you want to react and then do it.

Never be afraid to look at yourself objectively. It is impossible to know completely and understand yourself at all times, and so this is a never ending cycle of learning. Ask your most trusted friend to analyze you and tell you what they think your weaknesses and strengths are. Look for any obvious patterns in their comments and do not criticize their comments or judge them. You asked for their input, and this will be a good practice in learning to control your emotions.

Keeping a daily journal or a diary is a good way to keep track of your progress and the things you still need to work on. At the end of every day write down some of the day's events, what feelings they created in you, and what you did to handle the situation. Look back over the writings periodically and see if you can see any overt patterns in the way you react to situations and events. Documenting your life events will make you more aware of how you react and the reactions you need to correct.

Know what motivates you to do your personal best. Every person has something in particular that keeps them going on even when others might have given up. The real problem is to keep your motivation firmly in your mind when the going is no longer smooth. Most people quit a project because they lose their personal motivation. Don't be one of those people. Don't lose sight of your goals and do not quit.

Don't forget to take time for yourself whenever possible. Life is exhausting at best, and when you become too worn down, you can't possible keep the level of effort you need to maintain forever. So take some time out to just be you. This will allow you to have the breathing room you deserve and will keep you from having undesirable emotional reactions to situations that don't warrant them.

Everyone has things that trigger them emotionally, and you are no different. People who are well aware of themselves have the ability to see their emotions when they happen. It is vital that you learn to be flexible with emotions and learn to put them into the situation. Never repress your emotions but do take the time to understand them before you let them escape.

Once you have learned to fully understand your own emotions and how they work for you, it is time to begin to manage your emotions so they will work for you even more intensely. This will mean being responsible for your physical wellbeing as well as your emotional wellbeing and learning to control and prevent those emotional outbursts.

Changing your sensory input is one sure way to help keep your emotions in check. Change things up physically by joining an exercise class or taking up a new game or sport. By putting your physical being into a new path, you will automatically cause changes in your mental state and that should be enough to shake up any dullness your brain might be feeling. And while you are taking up a new activity, make sure it fits into your schedule. If it does not, then do your best to make it fit. Keeping a schedule is the best way to ensure that all of your tasks are done completely and on time.

It is your special job to take care of yourself because you are the most important person in your life. Eating well and exercising when needed will go a long way toward keeping your body in the best possible condition. A healthy body houses a healthy soul and a healthy mind, and both of those are mandatory if you want to develop emotional intelligence.

Find productive activities to channel your energy into. When you experience emotions that are too overwhelming, it is perfectly okay to keep them hidden for a while. Not every emotion needs to find its way out. But the big ones will not stay buried for long, so learn to use them to fuel the energy needed to make you better at some other activity. And remember to be interested in the subject, no matter what it is. You may not think you will like it, but there is something interesting in almost every event or situation. Keeping an open mind is a good way to promote growth.

It can be difficult to establish trust with another person, but they will never trust you if they ever feel that you do not trust them. Trust that is broken or lost is hard to regain. Always try to keep in mind that people are human and humans will make mistakes. When you offer to keep trusting them even though they act humanly, then you are giving them an invitation to give you their trust in return.

You should always have personal goals. When you have accomplished a goal make a new one. You should always have a new desire, a new goal, on the back burner waiting for a spot to open up. Emotional intelligence, just like life, is not a destination but a continuous journey. Make your goal reflect both your strengths and your weaknesses; all areas of your life need constant work. And always make sure that your goals are realistic and have clear methods for achieving them. When you achieve your goals, your self-confidence rises and higher self-confidence causes you to strive to set your goals.

Keep your mindset optimistic and positive. There are no failures but rather learning opportunities. Keep yourself surrounded by positive, optimistic people. It will rub off on you. Avoid people with negative mindsets.

Never lose an opportunity to remain in a learning mode. Information and knowledge are there to feed your mind and keep your motivation and curiosity alive. These days, information is easy to find anywhere you look, so there is always a chance to fuel your passions and your values. The biggest challenge to your continued learning might be getting out of your personal rut. When people become stuck on one mindset, they fail to grow and develop. Commit to learning new truth and new sills no matter how much effort it takes. Don't be afraid to grow. Challenge your thoughts as often as possible.

Everyone needs help eventually. No one person is omnipotent. So do not be afraid to ask others for assistance every now and then. And when other people ask for your help, help them whenever possible. Asking for assistance takes a big shot of fortitude so if you must turn someone down try to do so as kindly and gently as possible. Always be mindful of the other person's feelings.

To be able to truly empathize with other people, you need to be able to understand what another person is really saying. This means that you need to truly listen to the words the other person is saying and not just the sound of their voice. Let other people speak without interrupting them. Do not have preconceived notions about where the conversation is going. Really listen to the other person with an open heart and not skepticism. Put your own issues aside and give yourself the time to fully take in the events of the situation and think how that other person is feeling before you allow yourself to react.

And it does not matter if you are a team member or a team leader, you must always be involved and ready to help where needed.

If you truly need to do so to fully understand the other person better, try to take their emotion as your own and truly feel it inside. Be them for a while. See the world from their viewpoint. There is often no wrong or right in a situation—the only difference being the point of view of the person in the situation. And a quick way to build rapport with another person is to share a similar event or situation in your own life. This will mean opening up your vulnerabilities, but this is not only how you connect with other people, but it is also how you grow and learn.

People who excel at empathy are extremely curious about all people. Don't keep your conversations locked up in your little social circle. Talk to strangers whenever possible. Learn about other people and what makes them tick. This is not the time to be hesitant or shy. You will need to really put yourself out there to be able to connect with many other people because some people will meet you halfway and some will not. But by talking to many different people, you will expose yourself to different lives, views, and opinions that you may never have heard before. And when you are listening to these new people talk, make it very clear that you are listening. Nod your head, smile, say "yes, I see" as often it seems legitimate to say.

Social skills are vital for emotional intelligence as they are those particular skills that are needed to handle and influence the emotions of other people. Social skills cover an enormous range of personal abilities, from conflict management to dealing with change to communicating well with others. Building relationships and meeting new people is an integral part of everyday life, from your romantic lives to your work life.

One good way to begin improving your social skills is to take one skill you already know you would like to develop and learn to develop it. This could mean anything from taking a class to finding someone who is good at that particular skill and asking for advice. And this includes practicing your social skills. To do this, you need to get off the computer and out into the world. These kinds of social skills require seeing people face-to-face. Yes, it can be scary but it is an exercise that is well worth it. You don't need to just go out in public alone the first time. Use a reasonable excuse to get out among other people. Take a class, go to a seminar, have coffee after work with a coworker. Every little step will open you to larger and longer personal meetings. And this is the best way to grow your social skills.

Always be mindful of what your body is doing while you are around other people. Nonverbal communication can be more important than verbal communication because it is usually more honest. It is easy for people to mentally censor what they plan to say, but sometimes the body tells other people things that the mouth keeps hidden. Eye contact, tone of voice, and body language all talk volumes, and they let other people know what your current emotional state is. Body language is one area you need to learn to control to be able to develop a higher level of emotional intelligence.

Not every learning on the path to emotional intelligence is something positive. As with anything else, there are always things you will need to avoid. People who desire emotional intelligence learn to avoid drama at all costs. They have no place in their lives for other people's drama, either real or contrived. If someone truly needs help or advice, an emotionally intelligent person will offer what they can, but they will not take the other person's problems on as their own.

It is rare for an emotionally intelligent person to feel or act like a victim. When people complain about circumstances or situations, it means that they see no solution to their individual problem and that they feel like victims. Not only do emotionally intelligent people refuse to feel like victims but they would never even suggest that they would not be able to come up with a reasonable solution to the problem. They will never look for something or someone to blame but they will always look for a solution.

Cynical thoughts have no place in the mind of the emotionally intelligent people. They realize that negative thoughts exist but they acknowledge them as just that—negative thoughts. They rely on facts and analysis to discern a proper conclusion to the problem and then they keep their chosen course until the problem is solved.

Those people who possess a higher level of emotional intelligence choose to learn from the choices and mistakes they have made and not in dwelling on the past in a negative way. They are mindful enough to live in the present and not in the past.

Try to consider the needs of other people and not be too selfish in your wants and desires. Remember that other people have wishes and desires too, and yours are not the only ones that matter. Too much personal selfishness will erode relationships and cause a drop in social skills. And never think you need to automatically do what your friends are doing just to keep them as your friends. That idea needs to be left in elementary school. Peer pressure is only a good thing if it pushes you to do something good and positive with your life.

Being overly critical with other people is the quickest way to make an enemy or to crush someone else's self-esteem. Everyone has feelings just like you do. Everyone has the limitations and motivations that you do. Communicate carefully the changes you need to see and be careful to spare the other person's feelings whenever possible.

Aspiring to a life of emotional intelligence will change your life dramatically. It will allow you to learn to manage your own emotions in an effective manner. If you can change the way you feel about a situation, then you can change the way you feel about a situation. Do not automatically jump to conclusions when you feel things are not going the way you think they should go. Remember that most people create an action based on them and not on you. Do not be afraid to be rejected because if you are, you will not put yourself out there and you will never develop any skills. Being successful means failing sometimes. But look at those failures as challenges and opportunities for growth. Stress is a part of life. How you chose to handle it is the key to your success. You should always be proactive and not reactive. The proactive person has a plan in place for something that might happen. The reactive person has to quickly scramble to create a plan when something happens. Proactive people prepare, and reactive people are not prepared. Try never to be reactive but always try to be proactive. Be sure to understand the difference between assertive and rude. Rudeness is cold and unfeeling and does not take into account the other person's feelings. Assertive means, to go after what you want but always being mindful of the feelings of other people. And never feel guilty about going after what you want as long as you do it with grace and empathy.

The traits that bring emotional intelligence will evolve over time, just as long as you personally have the desire to keep it growing and evolving. Every situation, challenge, or person you face is another opportunity to put your emotional intelligence to the test. Possessing a higher level of emotional intelligence will be your best ally in work and in society. It takes a lot of practice, but you can do it. By successfully applying all the traits of emotional intelligence and understanding what it will mean to you and your life, you can reach your goals and achieve your full potential.

Conclusion

Thank you for making it through to the end of *Emotional Intelligence for Women* by Donna Mayer. Let's hope it was informative and able to provide you with all of the tools you need to achieve your personal goals whatever they may be.

The next step is to take the information that you have read in this book and use them to improve your life and begin your journey to emotional intelligence. This is your time to shine in the world, and you need to take this opportunity and run with it. Take the guidance that is in this book and use the information to set new goals for yourself and plan the path you will take to reach them.

Finally, if you found this book useful in any way, a review on Amazon is always appreciated!

Description

Women want to be a larger and more important force in the working world, but there is so much going against them that it seems like an impossible task sometimes. Strides have been made and the tide is beginning to turn, but there is still work to do. And much of that work will be dependent on women themselves to step up to the plate and make the changes that are necessary to make them game players in the world of business.

In this book, *Emotional Intelligence for Women* by Donna Mayer, women will learn the skills that they need to possess in order to achieve the emotional intelligence that will take them to the next level and beyond. Women have waited in the shadows for far too long, and it is time for them to take control of their lives and their careers.

Developing emotional intelligence is the way women will achieve their dreams and goals. From learning to exactly what emotional intelligence is, to learning how to develop it, this is the book every woman with big dreams needs to read.

Of course, people want to know if women are naturally more emotionally intelligent than men are, and that point is discussed in the book. The natural gifts that women already possess that will start them on their way to emotional intelligence are part of the ability that will give women the edge they need to succeed.

You will learn how to use emotions to create emotional intelligence. You will also see how emotional intelligence will take women into leadership positions and keep them there. After all, women have been controlling their emotions and exhibiting self-control for centuries. This book will teach them how to take that control and transform it into a strength that will benefit them greatly in the business and the social world.

Because social skills are mandatory to great leadership, these are discussed in depth. And the many ways that emotional intelligence can lead to better health, wellness, and relationships is covered inside.

This is the book for any woman who wants to better herself for any reason, whether it is to achieve advancement at work or to live a more fulfilled life. This is the only book she will ever need to help her achieve all of her goals.

www.ingramcontent.com/pod-product-compliance
Lightning Source LLC
Chambersburg PA
CBHW072232170526
45158CB00002BA/860